Guide Dogs

More Amazing Dog Tales

Edited by
NEIL EWART

RINGPRESS

© Ringpress Books & Neil Ewart 2005

First published in 2005 by Ringpress Books,
a division of Interpet Publishing,
Vincent Lane, Dorking, Surrey RH4 3YX
United Kingdom

British Library Cataloguing in Publication Data
A CIP record for this book is available
from the British Library

ISBN 1 86054 249 2

Cartoons by
RUSSELL JONES

The content of this book does not necessarily reflect the views
or current practice of The Guide Dogs for the Blind
Association, the author or publishers

Foreword

Mike Mullan

It is claimed that the dog is man's best friend; it should also be that man is the dog's best friend. Unfortunately, this is not always so.

Dogs tolerate man's moods, sometimes harsh handling and even neglect, will always respond in a positive way to a kind word, or to the slightest show of affection – even after distasteful treatment. They read our moods, comfort us when we are down, and help maintain our health by taking us out for exercise!

Man can prove to be the dog's best friend by ensuring that he is brought up to be a good citizen, with good social habits, basic training, correct diet and regular health checks. Physical and mental exercise is also very important; the dog that is taken out to run free, chase a ball or a frisbee, play hide-and-seek, and do a couple of play recalls, will be a more stable and reliable companion without 'behavioural' problems – and will repay all this love and care by being, in return, man's best friend.

I am sure that this second volume of *Amazing Dog Tales*, compiled by Neil Ewart, will be as successful as the first volume (published in 2003), and will help to raise the much-needed funds for training guide dog partnerships.

I have known Neil for well over 20 years, and consider him a close friend. During this time I have admired his unstinting work, not only in his professional capacity within The Guide Dogs for the Blind Association, but also for his concern for the well-being of all dogs.

The respect of his knowledge and appreciation of his friendship is reflected by the huge response when Neil requested input for *More Amazing Dog Tales* from his many friends and acquaintances in the wonderful world of dogs. It will be fun to read, as well as highlighting some of our human weaknesses and mistakes that might affect our best friend – the dog.

Introduction

Neil Ewart

I must first thank all those individuals and organisations for their contributions to this, the second book of anecdotes.

It is very difficult to fully express the joys and occasional tribulations that owning dogs presents us with. However, I recently acquired a letter sent to a Captain Liakhoff, who was in charge of training guide dogs in the UK from the 1940s through to the early 1960s. It is simply signed A.H.F. I hope you agree that the writer really has got to the heart of the matter:

A year or two ago, before I took an active interest in the work of guide dogs, I fell into conversation with a man who had lost his sight in the war, but with the aid of a trained guide dog was employed in a useful job and leading a full, interesting and happy life. At the time I met him, he was doing the family shopping in a busy town and seemed only too pleased to answer my questions about his dog.

Before parting, I apologized for detaining him, saying I was sure he must become very bored with constant questions about the dog. His reply, which summed up in a sentence what the dog really meant to him, impressed me so much that I have wished ever since that every sightless person could possess one of these invaluable dogs.

"Bored," he said, "but why? Most people are conceited enough to want to talk about themselves and I am no exception. However, I am never tired of talking about my dog, because my dog is me!"

Read and enjoy.

GOD BLESS ME

Carys M. Bannister, OBE

A few years ago, I was working as a consultant surgeon in one of Manchester's larger hospitals, and I was privileged to be allowed to take my Corgi, Megan, with me to work.

The plans to enlarge the hospital were well underway with the building of phase one, a large square, chunky, three story edifice, still awaiting the construction of its outer walls.

As I was walking Megan down to the car park, my thoughts were faraway when my attention was caught by the sound of God Save the Queen, whistled melodiously, floating across the driveway to me.

I glanced across to see a workman on each of the floors of the building standing to attention and saluting.

I did my best to give them a Royal Wave, only to be greeted by a chorus of male voices saying: "God bless you, Queen Mother!" I was quite taken aback.

I shouted to them: "I don't mind being mistaken for Her Majesty the Queen but, please, not the Queen Mother."

At the time the Queen Mother, God bless her soul, was nearing her 100th birthday!

The workmen must have thought I was the oldest looking female surgeon in the country. I know surgery is a stressful occupation – but not that stressful…

JOURNEY FROM HELL

Chris Muldoon, Australian guide dog instructor

There are many dogs I have trained that bring a smile to my face. But there are a few others I remember because they didn't make it.

One such dog was the mighty Jarvis, who was not to be outdone by his brother Jarman – a terrible twosome that wrought havoc on all who trained them. Jarvis was allocated to me to train, and from the moment I looked into the dog run and saw him, I felt things were not going to go well.

He was sitting by himself while all the other dogs were playing, and when I looked at him a clear understanding about rights of entry was established. I could come in if he was OK about it. Jarvis was a dog's dog in every sense of the word. A Labrador Retriever by birthright, but a Great Dane mentally and in dimension. His body was a couple of sizes too big for him, and he knew it!

He, by an uncanny understanding of vectors, sheer power to weight ratios and application of force against force, could turn a simple training walk in harness into the famous Iditarod cross-country sledge pull. On a wet day a Guide Dog Cadet Instructor such as myself could come back to the office with the left arm that holds the harness noticeably longer and lacking in function for the rest of the day.

What made it worse for me was that Jarvis knew this and loved it. It was all part of life's rich tapestry for him – pitting of dog against human was his mantra and his numerous victories over me were sweet nectar to be savoured in the process. It was, by definition, fun to run me ragged – and then watch my frustration. A blissful interlude was to see me whipped around a corner like a water skiing champion on a barefoot slalom, and glorious ecstasy to crash me into every overhanging tree and bush that, with a slight step to the left, might have been avoided.

The Scot ancestry in me came out and, with the resolution born of a national heritage that has seen us thumped a thousand times by everyone who has visited our country since the Roman occupation, I gritted my teeth and set about the challenge. I told my boss, John, that we would work it out, that we would learn each other's tolerances and grow into a team. John could obviously see the humour in this ludicrous belief and left me to turn Jarvis into a guide dog.

Our favourite game was "you put your left foot in" – a variation on the popular dance hall song called the Hokey Cokey. As we approached a kerb, the general rule for a guide dog is that the dog must come to the join of the kerb and the road. On reaching the join, the dog must place its feet as close to the edge of the kerb as possible, indicating there is a stop to be made.

For Jarvis this action was an opportunity to play mind games, and to show me, in no unclear fashion, that he made the decisions in this team. We would carefully approach a kerb and, fearing the habitual game, I would warn Jarvis I would not accept errors.

"Careful, careful Jarvis up to the kerb, there's a good lad."

Jarvis would draw me into the game by stepping

cleanly up to the kerb with a great demonstration of his alleged care and concern about not stepping over. Just when he knew I was about to say "good boy", he would, while looking straight up at me, place his right front foot squarely into the road. Round one, seconds out, let the fight begin.

"No! bad boy, don't do that again," I would growl at him, with implied threat in every syllable. For emphasis and to demonstrate how important it was to get this right, I would walk back five paces, turn him around and approach the kerb again. On the second attempt, he was perfection personified, like there had never been a problem. Merrily we would continue along the street until the second road crossing. The same pre-emptive support: "be careful, go carefully, Jarvis" – the same feigned interest in getting it right, showing all manner of concern and fear of transgressing the rule about kerb approaches. As we stood perfectly aligned with the kerb and the footpath, I felt we had connected. A millisecond before I gave Jarvis his praise, not only for getting it right, but for abandoning the game, he would, with meticulous cruelty, look up at me and place his left foot in the road.

And so the Hokey Cokey went all round the streets of North Balwyn to the undying mirth of other instructors. With head bowed in shame I watched as they would come out on breaks to see Jarvis perform his dance with me on the kerbs. Some days Jarvis got sick of the game, and for variation would literally launch both feet on to the road as the ultimate defiance. "I'm gonna do it and you try and stop me". Round and around we would go. On some days Jarvis would alternate strategies, obviously to relieve his boredom with the task, luring me into a false sense of security. On one street crossing he would approach it with consummate care and do it perfectly, then on the next (chortling merrily to himself I have no doubt), he would Hokey Cokey again.

The end for Jarvis as a prospective guide dog came about half way through his training. Part of the guide dog's training involves travelling on public transport, and it was at this time that we decided to tackle buses. To everyone's amazement, including my own, Jarvis saw this as an opportunity to excel. He found the door of the bus easily, took the necessary care to allow me to get on safely, and found me a seat every time with flawless determination. I was so impressed with Jarvis that I would tack on to other instructor's travel sessions on buses. I would show them how good he was at negotiating public transport, and how by my perseverance and support the big fellow had turned the corner.

On the fateful day I was working with Pete McNabb and his dog Banjo, travelling the local bus route in and around the Kew area. We had got on without incident, with Jarvis doing his best impression of a guide dog, and even though the driver was a bit erratic Jarvis was taking it in his stride. I was watching the little driver's face in his rear view mirror and it was clear that he didn't know quite what to make of this big dog sitting on the floor of the front seat behind him, looking back into the body of the bus. In fact the more he was watching in his rear view mirror, the less he concentrated on the road ahead, and we squealed around some of the usually more sedately driven corners in Kew.

"The driver doesn't like dogs," said Pete, "He was really jumpy yesterday, too."

"Oh good," I said. "Jarvis is all he needs to contend with to compound his fears."

Dogs have an uncanny way of assessing fear and Jarvis had the poor little driver summed up in a flash. Now not only was I watching Jarvis in the rear view mirror, but so was Jarvis. The speed increased.

I didn't notice it as we sped along, but another factor was looming on the horizon, one that was to put the icing on the cake. Like a storm a long way off, the disaster was coming.

A young lad of about fifteen had got on the bus with a golf bag over his shoulder. He sat directly opposite Jarvis and myself, and gave the dog a bit of a look. Seeing the harness he made no attempt to interact with the dog, but gave me a look like "how come you're not blind," but he didn't follow up with the usual questions. I put this acceptance down to good manners, and an understanding that guide dogs should not be touched or talked to at any time.

The lad placed the golf bag full of clubs in front of his feet, upright so the heads of the clubs were near his head, and began to be distracted by events outside the window. At my feet, where Jarvis was sitting, there began a low rumbling like the bus was going over corrugated iron. When I looked down the hackles on Jarvis were fully erect, and he had riveted his gaze on to the golf bag. I looked across and saw to my horror what he was showing aggression towards. In the golf bag were a number of clubs with head covers on them. The club covers were in the form of what could be described as cute cartoon characters and little animals, some with fluffy heads and some with little arms.

As the bus driving equivalent of Jackie Stewart became more distressed, it became apparent that it was because he could hear this rumbling from Jarvis. As the big dog began to growl audibly, he unconsciously applied more throttle to the already heaving bus. This, in turn, made the little club headcovers in the bag dance a jeering tarantella in front of poor Jarvis. The little heads with plastic, unseeing eyes were staring back with a mad vacancy at Jarvis, who was trying to give them his best "stop staring at me" look.

The faster we went, the more the heads danced; the more Jarvis felt he was losing control, and the more I knew I didn't have any. My gentle soothing of the dog and applied tightening of the leash were now nothing more than secondary irritation. I saw the headlines "guide dog eats golf bag on bus" and saw my career slipping away from me. As I gripped on for dear life, the storm broke and Jarvis sat bolt upright and gave the most thunderous bark at the bobbing heads in the golf bag. Their little fluffy tops and arms were goading him on to greater volume as we tumbled around, while Jackie Stewart tried to get further away from the problem by driving faster. The barking got even louder, this sent the bus driver into a panic, which threw everyone around in the body of the bus, creating more problems as the clubs began to lift out of the bag. This seemed to Jarvis an overt attempt to have a go at him, as they got suddenly bigger and were now coming for him. Like Custer at the Little Big Horn, he sounded the charge in a baleful wolf-like howl and stood to his full height, with me on the end trying for all I was worth to hold him back.

The lad took this look and stance as an act of

Grrrrrrrrrrr!

aggression from Jarvis personally, and attempted to cower behind the bag, shoving it further away from him, and closer to the now furious Jarvis. The whites of the driver's eyes could be seen clearly as big, round saucers in the rear view mirror – he hadn't taken them off the events in the bus for a while. I could see the thought processes he was putting together as if they were written on his face. Confucius says if mad dog eats all the fluffy heads of the golf clubs then the next thing that looks a bit like a fluffy head in a golf bag is going to be eaten, too – and that is the person driving the bus. He was jabbering and gesticulating wildly, which did nothing for his control of the vehicle and the situation in general.

We ground to a halt at the next bus stop, and with little ceremony, Jarvis and I were bundled off the vehicle, with him still trying to get at the little heads by baying and barking at them. Like a drunk in the pub who wants to fight the bar, he wanted the little heads to take the matter outside where he could get at them. As he stood on his back legs, I got the full picture of just how big Jarvis was – he was every inch equal to my six foot. I looked at the ashen faces of the other passengers, wondering if it was the events or the driving that had them looking like train wreck survivors. I decided it was Jarvis, the Hound of the Baskervilles, that was the catalyst.

With the driver still gesticulating wildly – and the heads in the golf bag waving goodbye – I looked for the face of my colleague, Pete, who was still on the bus. As the dust followed the bus away in a final pit stop, I watched Pete, and any chance of Jarvis becoming a guide dog rolled away like the tears of laughter streaming down Pete's face.

A WEIGHTY PROBLEM

Norman McIver, guide dog instructor

One of the guide dogs I trained lived in Colchester. Inexplicably, Kye started to put on weight, and his family became quite concerned as there was no obvious reason. He was having the correct amount of food and no titbits. The vet was consulted, but he could not find a reason.

A plan was formulated to spy on him during the evening when he was supposed to be asleep. Husband and wife prepared for bed, but the wife hid two-thirds up the stairs. After 15 minutes, Kye was

observed waking up, looking around, then sneaking out of his bed and into the kitchen, where he raided the cat's bag of food. Problem solved.

BEDSIDE MANNER

Ruth Bending, guide dog owner

Robyn and I have been working together since 2000. She is my first guide dog. I lost my sight in 1998 due to multiple sclerosis. Before I had Robyn, I never went out alone. Since training with Robyn, I have been able to start a college course, get involved with voluntary work, and have moved into my own flat to live independently. As well as my sight problems, my MS sometimes gives me trouble with walking. In 2002 I suffered a major relapse and had to learn to walk again. I was in hospital for three months, and Robyn came to visit me every day. She attended my physiotherapy sessions and really helped me get back on my feet. As well as being a very good working dog, she is a great friend and has helped me through many difficult times.

CHRISTMAS CRACKER

Wendy Jones, guide dog owner

For the first part of my life, I was unable to have a guide dog because of a severe phobia of dogs caused by an incident in my early childhood. I was never comfortable with the alternative methods of mobility and therefore, for many years, I very rarely went out alone and had to wait for other people's help to get anywhere. Eventually, after some therapy and help from a psychologist and Guide Dogs, I qualified with Becky in 1998. From the day I qualified, my life has never been the same. The freedom and independence she has brought is beyond my wildest dreams.

It was my dream to shop in Chester on my own, and the first Christmas that I was able to go with Becky and get my Christmas presents myself was one of the best Christmases ever. Because of Becky I can go to a doctor in private, buy gifts without people knowing and more. As a bonus, she has brought me love and companionship.

BUSTER-ED!

When efforts to make the southern Iraqi port of Umm Qasr operational again were being hampered by continual looting, Staff Sergeant Danny Morgan and his dog Buster were called in to help provide a search capability in the area. Here, Danny recalls the day when all their training paid off.

One day in April, I made my way to a pre-arranged grid reference and met up with some soldiers of the Duke of Wellington's Regiment who had requested a search dog for a planned operation. From there, two Land Rovers escorted me to their base location. It was a typically hot and dusty Iraqi day. I had not been this far forward before; come to think of it, none of us had.

After a little over an hour we turned off the main road and onto the usual sandy side-roads of Iraq, where occasional goats were tethered outside small farms on either side of the road. Once we'd reached the Duke of Wellington's camp, we went to the Op[eration]s tent for a detailed briefing. We were greeted by lots of smiling faces, and not just because we were there to support their operation. Buster seemed to bring a little normality to this strange situation, particularly to those who had dogs back at home.

That evening, it became apparent that our mission was to carry out a dawn raid on various houses in the town of Safwan, and disrupt the hold Saddam supporters had on the town. Intelligence had been gathered and houses had been identified and given code names in order of their priority of search. Times, locations, and the orders of march were confirmed. The raid was to be carried out the very next morning.

The convoy of vehicles departed at 03:00hrs and made its way to a grid reference just outside the town, ready to move at 05:00hrs, before the occupants of the target houses had had time to stir. The sun was coming up and the cool of the night would not last much longer. As we sat by the side of the road in our vehicles, we waited for the call sign, eyes on the target houses.

05:00hrs came and went with no word. The sun was getting higher in the sky and the temperature was rising. 06:00hrs came and went with still no word. Some of the locals were going about their business and the element of surprise was slipping away as we sat there – all 200 of us, in Land Rovers, lorries and armoured personnel carriers (APCs).

Finally, the word came to go. The convoy roared off like a big, sandy-coloured snake down the road towards the town. As we approached the houses, the APCs surrounded the area and the infantry secured the streets. A voice bellowed out in Arabic from a loud-haler on one of the vehicles, telling the occupants of the buildings to come out with their hands up. There was silence for what seemed like ages, although it was actually only a few minutes.

Nobody knew if the occupants were preparing to defend themselves or give themselves up. The voice boomed out in Arabic again, then more silence. Then there was movement at one of the gates: a woman dressed in only her nightclothes. The sight she saw must have scared her and she turned quickly back into the yard of the house, screaming and shouting. We didn't know what she was saying but she had left the locked gate open.

The infantry soldiers quickly made their move and ran into the yard, then the house. Soon, people were being escorted out: men, women and children. Once the houses were empty, the interpreter asked the occupants if they had any weapons in the houses. The reply was "no".

I beckoned my cover-man over before moving towards the houses and putting Buster into his harness to start the search. Buster made short work of the outside area and we soon entered the house. As Buster was keen to get on with the task at hand, I allowed him a free search of each room followed by a systematic search. As we entered one of the rooms I realised it was one of the best rooms in the house, but it was not occupied or used. Then Buster started to show interest next to a wardrobe; I could see his nose working overtime, and so was his tail. This was a thing I had seen many a time during training and I stood quietly, waiting for his reaction. Then it came: he sat at the base of the wardrobe, giving me an indication.

I instructed my cover-man to pass on the information to the soldiers outside. I called Buster out of the room and waited. An SNCO [senior non-commissioned officer] came into the house. I told him my dog had given me a positive indication by the wardrobe, but he informed me his men had looked inside the wardrobe but found nothing.

I wasn't happy. I trusted Buster with my life and he was so positive with his indication that I had to be as well. I told the SNCO I wanted it checked out again. He summoned two soldiers from outside who proceeded to search the room again. When they had opened the wardrobe and removed its contents, I asked them to look behind it. On moving the wardrobe, a piece of sheet tin which had been placed between the wardrobe and wall fell away. This exposed a purpose-built cavity, which revealed the barrel of a weapon. Buster's indication was confirmed.

I left the premises but waited to see what else would come out of the hide. Its contents included AK47 assault rifles, grenades, bomb-making equipment, hundreds of rounds, 2 kilos of cocaine and extremist literature. I would remember this day for the rest of my life. After years of training and handling dogs all over the world, we were at war and my dog and I had made our contribution. We had saved lives and we had trusted each other. This team had made a difference.

FLOOR SHOW

Robert Killick, canine author and columnist

Years ago when night clubs were smoke-filled, exotic rooms, with dimly lit tables and discreet waiters serving over-priced and over-rated champagne, gentle trios would play soft, seductive music to which lovers danced. At midnight and then again at 2am a cabaret would entertain – scantily dressed dancers would provoke single men, and a song and dance lady would sing love songs and move among the diners.

My wife, Jo, was one such lady, and she appeared with some success in many clubs around London. She bought an eight-week-old Toy Poodle, so small she could sit in the palm of her hand. Being a professional entertainer, Jo knew of the big 'Aaah' factor and was aware the effect a tiny puppy would have on the audience.

So, on the first night of a season, she appeared with it clutched to her bosom. After a few minutes the puppy, named Candy, grew restless. She looked so sweet with her diamante collar and silver lead that Jo put her on the floor so that she could be better seen. Candy immediately made a puddle about the size of a fifty pence piece. The audience fell about with laughter and applauded madly. Candy never forgot the applause and in 15 years working on various stages with Jo, she never failed to pee on her first entrance!

MOVE OVER FOR MACK

Jenny Moir, head of PR, Hearing Dogs for Deaf People

Mack is a Miniature Poodle who has been with his profoundly deaf owner, Edna Hind, for just over six months. He has already made a huge difference to her life, and has saved her from a terrible accident.

Edna and Mack were walking into town when they had to negotiate a narrow pavement on a blind corner. Just as they were rounding the bend, Mack suddenly gave a loud bark and pulled Edna sharply into the wall. Edna was surprised, as this was unusual behaviour for Mack, and she was just about to have some stern words with him when she saw a huge articulated lorry mount the pavement about six inches in front of her. With a shock she realised that had Mack not steered her away so quickly, the lorry would have crushed them both.

When Mack is not acting the hero, he can be a bit of a rascal. He has a huge personality for such a small dog, and makes a big impression on everyone he meets. However, there is one person who is not so pleased with Mack – and that is the vicar of the local church where Edna helps. She takes Mack every week and he sits quietly in the pew while she goes up to the altar. In fact, the only time that he moves is when he thinks the vicar's sermon has gone on long enough, and then Mack will stand up and peer at the vicar from the end of the pew as if to say: "That's enough now."

The vicar has learned to watch Mack's body language and times his sermons accordingly!

BREAD AND SHAM

Contents of a letter sent to Captain Liakhoff, Guide Dogs' first Director of Training, from a guide dog owner in the 1940s

Just at the end of the war there was no fresh meat to be had, and one day my guide dog went on strike. He refused to eat the tinned dog food which was all

I had, and which he always regarded as a very poor substitute for fresh meat. All day the hunger strike lasted, and by supper-time I was beginning to get a bit worried about my hard working dog that had eaten nothing.

Then I had a brain wave... the thing which delighted him above everything else was to try and beg any sandwiches which we might be eating. A tempting little pile of sandwiches was prepared, and to his great surprise, he was given them at the same time as we were all having our own supper. He ate them with very evident enjoyment.

I wonder if he ever realised that there was nothing in the sandwiches but tinned dog meat and very stale bread.

I'd rather eat gravel.

PEPPY POWER

Binnie Taylor, guide dog owner

When I was letting my guide dog, Peppy, into his run late at night, the back door to the sheltered housing shut, leaving us stranded with no keys, no harness or mobile phone.

Gently placing my right hand on the dog's back, we walked cautiously towards the main street, with no traffic for orientation. Peppy sensed the situation was somewhat unusual, and managed to slowly guide me across the road to a friend's house, where help could be summoned.

BIN THERE, DONE THAT

Norman McIver, guide dog instructor

Trainers from Dogs for the Disabled came to one of Guide Dogs' training centres to give a talk on their work. I asked them about some of their problems.

One story was about a lady who was a wheelchair user. Her dog was very good at retrieving, but became obsessive about items in a pedal bin! Eventually, the bin was put on a stand, which, in theory, put it out of the dog's reach. Not so! The dog still got in it, so the DfD trainer decided to put the bin in a box – but the dog quickly learned to open the box on the stand, and then get in the bin. So now the bin is on a stand in a box, which has a padlock on it!

It's only a matter of time!

ALARMING INCIDENT

Mike Mullan, dog trainer and Kennel Club member

In the 1970s and '80s we lived in a nice country area between Guildford and Camberley. It was quite an idyllic spot in which to live, although it did tend to attract burglars. At the time, we had four Dobermanns – a fact that was well-known in the area – and we felt that our home was relatively risk-free.

The neighbours were yachting fanatics and kept a large boat moored at Portsmouth. They left home most weekends, but they had a very sophisticated anti-burglar system, complete with alarms and blue flashing lights. They would leave us the key, and we generally kept an eye on things.

One Friday evening in September, they informed us that they were going to the boat for the weekend and they would be back Sunday evening. On the Saturday evening, at about 11.30 pm, I was putting the dogs out into the garden, before going to bed, when the neighbours' alarm shattered the quiet evening air with a vengeance. I immediately told Moira, my wife, to call the police and said I would go round with Barbie, my fully trained six-year-old Dobe bitch. I sent two other dogs back into my house, leaving Jimmy to keep an eye on things.

I quickly went next door, checking doors and windows – and nothing appeared to be open. Within a few minutes, a police car arrived. The alarm was still going off, and we could hardly hear ourselves speak. I suggested sending Barbie to quarter the large back garden. As the garden was laid out with ornamental bushes, greenhouses, etc, the policeman reluctantly agreed, but he obviously thought that Barbie was not actually a working dog. The dog was sent and, with reluctant admiration from the policeman, she quickly worked every bush and building – but turned up nobody.

While this was going on, Moira arrived with the front door key, plus an audience of a dozen neighbours from other properties who had been aroused by the din.

The policeman suggested that Moira unlock the door and go in to switch off the alarm. I instantly stopped this, saying "No way" – I was not prepared to put her at risk.

The policeman seemed a little reluctant to enter the building, and was pleased when I offered to send Barbie in first.

She was still hyped up from her search of the garden, and quickly headed through the now open front door, followed by me and the policeman. I commanded Barbie into the kitchen, through the dining room and into the lounge. The intolerable alarm was still going, so I did get Moira to switch it off.

I sent Barbie up the stairs and, within seconds of hitting the top landing, she was giving voice. My heart was in my mouth. The policeman was now halfway up the stairs, and I could barely command Barbie to leave, as I had no idea what she was barking at!

Downstairs we could hear the policeman speaking to someone. At first I thought it was the dog, but then realised he was getting a human response. I said to Moira that we had probably caught intruders when the policeman emerged with two very bewildered and sleepy owners of the house.

As it turned out, they had decided to return on the Saturday instead of the Sunday, and had gone straight to bed. How they didn't hear that darned alarm, I will never know. They needed some convincing that it had been going off for at least 20 minutes. Only when we advised them to look at the audience gathered outside, did they finally believe us.

Glancing at a very pleased Barbie, the policeman simply said: "They will never believe this at the station!"

CONFIDENCE BOOSTER

Karen Reed, guide dog owner

After my last dog was retired, I wasn't sure I would manage to retrain with a lively, young dog. I am Ramsey's second owner.

Sadly his first owner died, and Ramsey came to me two weeks prior to retraining. We bonded straight away, despite Ramsey having a lot of upheaval to contend with after losing his last owner.

His work is outstanding. Because I am physically disabled, my course is not always straight. He nudges me along, and supports me when I am tired. He has given me back my confidence. Socially he is superb, nothing fazes him. He is much loved wherever we go.

STEALING A MEAL IN COURT

Mike Mason, formerly with the West Midlands Police Dog Section

There were scary times in the 1970s working in Birmingham city centre with the bomb squad. I had a very trustworthy explosives dog known as Paddy the Pointer, who was well-known throughout the Midlands.

On this occasion, we were called out to a bomb alert at the law courts. When we arrived, the whole of the building had been evacuated and all the bigwigs were standing outside.

"Have you got a system for searching such a large building?" asked the officer in charge.

"Of course I have," says me. "It's called a good dog, coupled with good luck!"

Into the majestic halls we went – and I was amazed at the size of the building. We began the search, and after a while, in the very depths of the courts, I found a little man, in his court gowns, having a snooze in a small alcove. My dog gave him a nudge and a lick, and I asked what he was doing.

"I'm a jury bailiff" was his reply. "My jury are sitting and I'm guarding the door".

In disbelief, I opened the door to find a full jury sitting eating their lunch. My dog was now back on the lead beside me. One word – "Bomb" – and the whole jury did a runner, with me showing the way, followed by the bailiff pulling on my arm saying something about lunch and waving an empty Tupperware box.

Yes, Paddy had nicked his lunch plus clingfilm and an apple while I had been talking to the jury!

TOO HOT TO HANDLE

Janet Fairweather, fundraiser for Guide Dogs

Every year in the Richmond area we hold a sort of local 'Scrufts' Dog Show, which we call Capable Canines Day. June 2003 was particularly warm and, to our surprise, one dog handler was so hot that, without warning, she got into a paddling pool that had been put there for the dogs – fully clothed, with her dog...

SHORT CUT

Dave Stanton, guide dog instructor

Some years ago, when I was working as a guide dog mobility instructor at Leamington, we had a class of clients in for residential training.

One of the exercises we used to carry out was called 'drop-offs'.

This was performed towards the end of a class, and involved driving a group of clients and their new dogs to various points around the outskirts of Leamington town centre.

They would be 'dropped off', one at a time, and told to make their way to a given destination (usually a café), using the skills they had learnt during class training.

As I dropped off John, who was one of my clients, a fair way from the rendezvous, he asked me for a clue to help him get him underway. Not wanting to give him any particular advantage over the other members of the class, I simply said: "Just use your initiative, John".

We then dropped off the remaining clients at various points, before driving on ahead to the café, ready to greet people as they arrived. As we got to the café, I saw, to my amazement, that John was sitting at a table enjoying a coffee with his dog by his side!

When asked how he had managed to complete the task so quickly he replied: "Dave told me to use my initiative, so I jumped in a taxi!"

To the cafe my good man
and don't spare the horses!

MEMORABLE MUTTS

Nick Mays, Chief Reporter, Our Dogs

You know, it's a terrible confession for someone who works on a canine newspaper, but I never had a dog of my own until I was 26 years of age. Now I'm in my forties, I'd never be without one (or two, or three…).

The fact is, when I was a kid, I'd always wanted a dog, but my parents were resolutely against the idea.

I thought this was pretty unfair, as both had owned dogs when they were children, but I think they were wary of all the effort involved and the fact that the dog's upkeep would fall solely to them.

I promised I would feed the dog and take it for walks, but it was no good, they didn't bend. It even took them a long time to relent and let me keep hamsters, mice, rats and so on (but that's another story) – and it wasn't until I was 12 years old that I was allowed to have a cat. After that, we were never without one and we were on cat number three by the time I left home and got married. But in all that time, my parents remained firmly set on the 'no dogs' rule – and no amount of bribery and entreaties on my part made them change their minds.

However, I was a resourceful child – after all, my Dad's garden shed was square and black and vaguely resembled a police box, so that was, of course, the TARDIS (and guess who was Dr Who?). And, of course, a sizeable cardboard box made a good speedboat, or racing car, so making up for the lack of a dog of my own was easy – I used to borrow other peoples' dogs! Well… I say 'borrow' – I used to walk them, usually alongside the owners and later, when I was older, I would walk them on my own (and maybe reluctantly accept 50p for my trouble).

Quite a few people down my road kept dogs, and they kept them in a very simple, unfussy way as was the style in the late 1960s and early 1970s. I'm not saying the dogs all slept outdoors in old barrels or rickety wooden kennels, but they would all have the bones of the Sunday joint to chew on, table scraps to supplement their dog biscuits and tins of PAL, a tennis ball to chase, a rope 'tugger', and maybe a wooden toy dumbbell. Oh yes – and they deposited chalky-white dog poo, on account of the natural food diet – and a lot less of it than you find on the streets nowadays! (In fact, some of us rotten little horrors down my street would tell a big lad named Pete to show us how strong he was by picking up that white stone there and crushing it. Of course, it wasn't a stone…) In those days, I'm afraid, the dangers of toxoplasmosis weren't so well-known.

Interestingly, out of all those dogs, there was only one that was in any way 'dodgy' and that was Kipps, a very solid Corgi who did live outdoors – in a barrel. In his younger days, unfortunately, he wasn't averse to chasing kids down the street and taking a hefty nip at the postman.

Needless to say, any footballs that accidentally went into his owner's garden stayed there. Even in his old age, when Kipps toddled out into the street we would abandon our games of football, cricket or Pick Up That White Stone Pete and move to a respectful distance until Kipps had unhurriedly ambled past. I think the old scoundrel was about 20 years old when he finally passed away in his barrel (no doubt guarding a pile of footballs he'd nabbed over the course of his long lifetime).

I think the biggest canine influence in my young life, though, was my next-door neighbour's Boxer, Buster. He was middle-aged when Marie and Roy moved in next to us, but he retained a youthful outlook on life and enjoyed two or three walks a day, invariably down to the river. We lived in Mortlake, so the Thames flowed close by, and there were some wonderful dog walks along the towpath there. Of course, Mortlake is famous for three things: the Boat Race, brewing, and the tomb of the famous

Victorian explorer, Sir Richard Francis Burton.

Buster embraced two of these things full on. He wasn't fussed about the remains of famous explorers.

The Boat Race, however, was different – the one day of the year when there would be lots and lots of people down by the river. Buster became a dab hand at looking undernourished and cadging pieces of hot dog off visitors, and then submitting to all the patting and stroking, while Marie fielded daft questions as to whether he was a Bulldog or not ("No, he's a BOXER!"). Buster also liked the brewing and would often lap up beer that had been spilt along the towpath by Watney's brewery – and it was good cask beer for most of that time, none of that horrible keg stuff that came in later years. I think Buster would happily have lived in a barrel if it could have been a Watney's beer barrel! As it was, he sported a small Watney's red barrel key ring ornament on his collar – no doubt keeping brewing in the family.

Marie was a kind soul and would never object to me coming along for a walk with her and Buster. She would even let me hold his lead if she judged Buster was not in the mood to run off suddenly and see his girlfriend, the Poodle, owned by the landlord of the Ship, a pub along the road by the river. The usual signal for any disobedience on Buster's part was easy to spot – he would look at you sideways or over his shoulder, showing the whites of his eyes. Marie would exclaim: "Don't you dare show me the whites of your eyes!" to which Buster's response was usually to duck his head and look rather put out, as though saying "Me? Misbehave? How dare you Madam!" Or he would simply do whatever it was he was planning on doing and take a telling off later –

like the memorable time he found a bag of soggy buns washed up on the towpath. Despite Marie's protests, he scoffed them all down and then promptly vomited them up all over her feet.

What I realise about Buster now is that he was a good actor, and was extremely patient with me. He would put up with my childish antics, dive into the river to fetch sticks that I threw, and even pretend that I was in charge when I held his lead. If he'd had enough, he would let me know in subtle ways, just ignoring me, or putting on a special show of doggy defiance such as he showed me one day in Roy's car.

Roy worked at the brewery, and on Fridays he would finish a little earlier, so Marie, Buster and I would go to meet him after our walk, and then come back home in Roy's car. Now, don't ask me why, but Roy kept his car in a lock-up garage at the back of some flats by the river during the week. On Friday afternoons, he would drive the car home, park it outside his house and later he and Marie would use it to collect the weekend shopping, or to go on visits. It was just one of his quirks and it was all part of the Friday routine – walk Buster, meet Roy, collect car, drive home in car.

The only drawback was that, as a boy, I was terribly travel sick. Even the shortest of hops would have me heaving, unless I could stick my head out of the car window and get lots of fresh air. Trouble was, Buster also liked sticking his head out of the car window – and we both wanted to stick our heads out of the same back window… I don't think it ever occurred to either of us to use the opposite window.

One memorable Friday, Buster decided he'd had enough of being shoved out the way of the window by this impertinent child. I should have taken notice when he rolled his eyes at me and I saw the whites of them, but I thought he was just kidding ... until he used his powerful bulk to push me onto the back seat. When I protested and tried to push him off, he simply sat down on me and I was trapped. Struggling only made it worse, and I ended up face down on the back seat breathing in the smell of warm leather and protesting that I would be sick. Marie and Roy didn't intervene – they were yakking about some supermarket they were gong to.

How I didn't throw up, I don't know, but that five-minute journey from the garage to our road seemed more like five hours. When Roy parked outside our houses and opened the back door, Buster unhurriedly jumped out and I crawled out, sucking in lungfuls of fresh air and trying to control my stomach. After that little escapade, I respected Buster a bit more – he was, after all, many years my senior (in dog years as well as human years) so if ever we shared the back seat of the car, I always stuck my snout out of the opposite back window to Buster's. Or I would simply opt to walk home if Buster showed the whites of his eyes!

Mind you, he made up for sitting on me just a few weeks later in typical canine hero fashion. Being a horrible little boy, I loved carrying sticks around with me. They made great guns or spears, or, if I was in legend-mode, a Robin Hood quarterstaff. And you must have heard that old entreaty from parents: "You be careful with that stick or you'll have someone's eye out!" Well, one day I nearly did just that– and it was my eye.

I was messing around on the slippery towpath

with Buster when I slipped. The stick I was holding stuck in the ground and my face came down to meet it at speed – with the result that it scraped the side of my face, narrowly missing my eye. I still have the scar today. Well, I howled like a good 'un, but Buster was all over me, looking after me and generally doing his heroic rescue dog bit. If that red barrel on his collar had been bigger, he'd have proffered it to me, St Bernard-style for me to drink its restorative contents (presumably beer, not brandy). He sat close to me in the car ride home, putting his head next to mine as we both shared the same window to stick our faces out of. He even saw me to my front door when we got home.

Generally speaking, he had done as good an impression of Lassie as any Boxer could do. He may not have been Lassie, but he was good enough for me. One day, I shall have a Boxer of my own – and no prizes for guessing what I'll call him.

No, not Lassie…!

GIVING THEM THE EYE

Jenny Moir, head of PR,
Hearing Dogs for Deaf People

Robbie is a Spaniel cross, and together with his littermates he was donated for training as a hearing dog. He lives with his profoundly deaf owner, Nici Lowson, and has become a bit of a fashion icon.

When out and about with Nici, he proudly wears his burgundy hearing dog coat, but recently he swapped this for a very smart ceremonial Scottish jacket with a tartan edge when he was 'page-dog' at Nici's wedding.

He is already famous in Yorkshire, where he lives, and although he knows not to rush up to people when he is out with Nici, he has developed a foolproof way of getting them to say hello – he hypnotises them! He will focus on someone, staring at them while he wags his tail and looks pathetic and hopeful. Once he has eye contact, he wags his whole body frantically – still sitting – and the poor victim is hooked! It never fails.

When Robbie first went to live with Nici, he had

Look into my eyes .... You're feeling sleepy.

to get used to two other house guests – Nici's two cats, who, much to his surprise, kept disappearing through the catflap in the back door. For several weeks Robbie would use his hearing dog training to find Nici and alert her by touching, then lead her to the back door as if to say: "Look Mum – the cat went out!" The whole routine would happen again a few minutes later, but this time it was, "Look Mum – the cat's back!"

AMBER'S GREAT AMBITION

W. Jan Siuda, guide dog owner

My guide dog, Amber, sustained an injury to her shoulders and so she had to be retired early. She had to have two operations and was very brave, and her period of convalescence was a trial that she bore with fortitude.

During this time Amber wanted to guide me, and when her stitches were removed she wanted to go back in the harness. She was so brave that one day she tried to go on the lead to take me out. Amber heroically fought to gain her maximum fitness – and succeeded in getting back in the harness.

TELLY ADDICTS

Norman McIver, guide dog instructor

I visited a guide dog in Edinburgh to find it lying in front of the TV, intently watching the film Lassie.

Oh dear! Bobby-Joe's fallen in the mill pond again!

Another would love watching boxing on the TV, and would sway her head as if avoiding blows! No other programmes held any interest.

CREAM CRACKERS

Julia Barnes, writer

There are those that believe that Greyhounds are not the brightest of canines – but Blaze, a former racer, pulled off a stunt that made her Border Collie house-mate gawp in admiration.

Generally, Blaze found life to be a puzzle. She was used to kennels and the racing track, and she found country rambles and other family outings a mystifying experience. Zell, the Border Collie, would be miles out in front, playing complicated games of retrieve, and Blaze would trot along beside us, grinding to a halt if she came across an obstacle, such as a stile, which was more than she could cope with. If life got too difficult, she would resort to running oval-shaped laps of an imaginary racetrack – even if that meant encompassing a busy road … But every dog has its day, and Blaze was no exception.

The mystery started when we discovered that the bottles of milk left by the milkman had the top part missing. The silver foil tops were partially ripped, or in some cases, they had been completely removed. We thought long and hard, and the most likely explanation was that the ducks from the nearby pond had taken a helping. It seemed a bit unlikely – but we had heard of tits pecking at milk bottle tops – and we assumed that this was simply a duck version. We rather liked the idea of ducks waddling up to our door, and felt that we were enjoying life in country to the full.

But our dreams of caring for wildlife were rudely shattered when, one day, the milkman returned to his van, and paused for a few minutes to check some paperwork. He looked up – and Blaze was caught red-handed! One by one, she was neatly removing each milk bottle top in turn, and then using her long, pink tongue to suck up the milk.

From that day on, the milkman left the milk-crate on its side to thwart Blaze. But she clearly kept the trick in mind. Every time we went on holiday – to a Cornish village, with cottages sited around a green – Blaze would be up with the lark, to follow close on the heels of the milkman. As soon as he had completed his deliveries, she would visit every cottage in turn, stopping off for a refreshing drink of Cornish milk…

DON'T MESS WITH ME

Mike Mullan, dog trainer and Kennel Club member

Anyone who read about Ribs the Dobermann in the first book of Amazing Dog Tales, will be aware that she was a good, kind family companion who, by the age of six, had only once shown any form of aggression – and that was to defend my wife and daughter. At the end of that story I indicated that there was another time, some two years later, when Rib's natural guarding instincts came to the fore.

At the time I was general sales manager of a large garage in Uxbridge, and we generally had around 90 new vehicles in our storage area at the rear. This area backed on to a stream, and although it had an 8ft chain-link fence topped with barbed wire, we still experienced the theft of various car parts. We devised all sorts of observation schemes, including staying in the back of a one-ton van all night and, on occasions, arriving unexpectedly with my Dobe, Ribs, but always to no avail.

Then, one Sunday, I decided to call in and check around. I walked down to the car storage compound with Ribs off the lead. I allowed her to wander into the compound when, to my astonishment, within 30 seconds she started to give voice. I quickly followed the noise and, rounding the side of a van, I found Ribs standing guard over two very surprised youths who, from the evidence of equipment on the ground, were up to no good.

Ribs was standing facing them, daring them to move. I called her back to me, and then told the youths to walk back to the office where I intended calling the police.

At this request I received a volley of verbal abuse, and the larger one made a move towards me. This was a big mistake, as Ribs immediately turned into protection mode and leapt towards him. Fearing the worst, I yelled: "Leave". She obeyed instantly, missing the youth by a thousandth of an inch. She then insisted on standing between me and the pair until the police arrived and both youths were taken into custody.

The managing director of the garage was particularly delighted at the outcome because he had persuaded me to take on Ribs three years earlier, when her previous owners could no longer keep her at their pub in Canterbury.

DEBT RELIEF

Beverley Cuddy, Editor, Dogs Today

Although I have had several lovely dogs since, Sally was such a huge character that she is central to nearly all my doggie anecdotes. She was a gorgeous fawn Bearded Collie – the rarest colour – a real champagne blonde. Sally was a pup at that horrible time when parvovirus was raging, and there was still no really effective vaccine. We took all the usual precautions but she still got it. If you have never seen a dog with parvo, you are very lucky. My mother and I nursed Sal at home. Our vet said that if she hospitalised her on a drip, she may become depressed and just give up. If we could keep her spirits up, it would give her a better chance of survival.

Around the clock, every 15 minutes, we took turns to syringe fluids down her mouth. We kept a detailed log as to how quickly she vomited after a dose. Once a day we took her to the vet for a painful injection into the muscle in her neck that would slow the dehydration. We measured her survival chances on the strength of her screams. On days when she just whimpered, we got very down. The nightmare went on for days and days, and she soon became a pathetic, limp, furry bag of bones. She lay on our laps exhausted – but she still managed a little wag when we talked to her. She even greeted the vet every day, despite how she had to hurt her.

Sally certainly had spirit. The gaps between being sick suddenly lengthened. Against the odds, she had beaten parvo. But life couldn't get straight back to normal. She had to remain apart from other dogs until she stopped being a risk to them. By then Sally had missed all her vital socialisation – and she had only experienced pain from those strangers she had met. Sally grew into the most beautiful dog I had ever known, but she was usually cripplingly shy. She would peep at people from a distance – curious but terrified. A canine Bambi, her devotion to me was extreme. She couldn't bear to be apart – she was the personification of the very worst case of separation anxiety. If she became stressed, the results were almost always the same. She would evacuate her bowels without warning. Now sometimes this was not very convenient. Once, however, it was a bonus.

Sally went everywhere with me – including work. In the early days of Dogs Today things were far from glamorous. I had done a management buy-out of the title, and things were rather hand to mouth. Sally made me feel safe when I worked long hours alone at the office. She was always there with a reassuring head on my knee when I had a difficult phone call to make. At one time we had more dogs than people in the office.

I had a substantial bad debt to chase, and I had asked the offending advertiser to come in to see me and discuss settling his account. He was rather an abrasive chap, a bit of a bully. He was trying to get me to wipe his debt and take products in lieu of money. I was very loathe to do this – but he was very forceful. I was on the point of buckling just to get rid of him. But I hadn't realised I had the best credit control assistant in the world – Sally. She calmly stood up, turned her bottom in his direction, moved her tail to one side and sprayed him with pungent diarrhoea. He turned green, but he got his cheque book out instantly and paid in full!

Ready - Take aim - Fire!!

Sally memories always make me smile. We had 16 amazing years together – liberally peppered with less fortunate emissions – but her companionship definitely enriched my life in many ways.

LOVING SUPPORT

Jane Bowden, guide dog owner

As well as being totally blind, I have a congenital back problem, which is worsening with age and is, at times, excruciatingly painful.

On my worst days, when I still go out with Esmi for our walk, she slows right down to a pace I can cope with. This magnificent dog also returns to normal speed, which can be quite quick, on my best days. Besides this, when I rise from the kneeling position after grooming her, she arches her back so I can press lightly on her to steady myself as I stand. She truly is a god-send.

COAL MERCHANT

Norman McIver, guide dog instructor

Guide dog Ember was appropriately named – he loved lying in front of an open fire with his front legs stretched out in one direction and his back legs the other way. Curiously, one of his favourite pasttimes was to attempt to bury coal around the house. Being a very light-coloured yellow Labrador, he ended up looking like a Dalmatian!

SPYING ON SOAPY

Jenny Moir, head of PR,
Hearing Dogs for Deaf People

Little Ted is a five-year-old Papillon. He is a hearing dog for his owner, Chris Hart, and has a best friend in the shape of a cat called Soapy.

Soapy and Ted are very close, and Ted sometimes forgets he's a dog and thinks he's a cat. His favourite toy is a red soft toy mouse, and he loves playing hide and seek with this – just like a cat! When he is not telling Chris about sounds, or playing with his red mouse, Ted enjoys nothing better than playing with Soapy.

Ted has been trained to tell Chris about sounds in the home by finding him and scrabbling at him with his paws, then leading him to the source of the sound. Ted absolutely loves his work as a hearing dog – so much so that Chris has now realised that Ted has even combined his hearing dog training with his games with Soapy! He found this out when Ted came one day to touch him, and Chris asked: "What is it?" thinking it was a genuine sound. Ted then led him into the kitchen where there was a real mouse, which Soapy had brought in! Since that first time, Ted has alerted Chris to a live bird in the hall, and a wild rabbit in the lounge – all brought in by Soapy!

Being a Papillon, Ted has beautiful, large, butterfly ears, and very sharp hearing – and is constantly listening out for things to tell Chris about. With Soapy joining in the fun, there is never a quiet moment in the Hart household!

HOW IT ALL STARTED

Neil Ewart, author

There has always been some speculation about how man and dog first formed a partnership which has lasted over thousands of years. Experts believe that man would have seen the dog's ability to hunt its prey and, wisely, spotted the chance to save a lot of footwork. It is also likely that dogs would have smelt food, either being cooked, or thrown out of the cave for collection by the local authority. If they played their cards right, they could actually give up catching prey themselves and this strange two-legged beast could supply their needs.

However, allowing for the fact that nothing much really changes over time, I would like to put forward a much more likely scenario.

Picture, if you will, a typical scene in a cave overlooking a very rural Hounslow Heath. Mr and Mrs Ug had been married for some time, and as Mr Ug was not now looking for a wife they had named their home Dun Clubbin'.

It was Christmas Day, and Mr Ug had just returned from his local a little worse for wear. (I must add here for the purists that neither the Ugs, nor anyone else for that matter, knew it was Christmas for many thousands of years, but you get the drift!)

He was a key member of the local spear team at a rough sort of pub appropriately named The Cave Inn. This differed from modern day darts teams, as the lads did not use a board to throw at, but aimed at each other. Also, the 'darts' were a bit bigger than those seen today.

On his arrival home, Mrs Ug pointed out in no uncertain terms that his brontosaurus steak was burnt to a cinder and that it was time he changed their cave paintings as they were the same ones that had been there when they married.

Also, her mother was coming to stay, and she could not be expected to live in such squalor. At that point Mr Ug gazed thoughtfully at a painting of a large, hairy bison, but wisely refrained from saying what came into his head.

Reluctantly, he retreated to the back of the cave and commenced scraping some old paint off, when voices outside announced that Tracey and Darren Ug, their children, had returned from the Druids' Sunday School. Mr Ug could hear lots of "Oohs" & "Aahs" coming from Mrs Ug, and upon investigation, he saw a pair of eyes and a small black nose peering out of Tracey's loincloth.

It was a wolf cub....

"Look what we've found, Dad," she trilled. 'It's lost its mum."

Mr Ug went cold. "Well take it back and its mum will find it," he pleaded.

"But Dad, we promise to look after it. We will walk it and clean up when it makes a mess in the cave."

(See, nothing really changes over the years!)

Mr Ug instinctively knew he had already lost the argument.

"We can't afford it," he said feebly, and immediately regretted mentioning money.

Mrs Ug retaliated by pointing out the amount he

Just taking the wolf for a walk, Dear.

just spent on a wheel – and what was the use of just one wheel – and that she had not had a new outfit for years, and that the neighbours always had several holidays a year at the new holiday camp opened by a B. Butlin, known as Stonehenge. (And you thought it was there for the summer solstice.)

Knowing he was beaten, Mr Ug returned to the back of the cave to resume his scraping. So, the first pet dog was established. Meanwhile, a neighbour spotted a chance to make a more comfortable living, so he quickly moved to a much bigger cave and opened a Vet's Surgery.

Within a few weeks, Darren had become a little over-friendly with the daughter of a neighbour who lived in a district that Mrs Ug did not approve of – "a load of barbarians!"

Tracey had spotted some wild ponies, and also had become rather keen to listen to groups of hairy lads who played music down the local amphitheatre. She had covered her newly painted cave paintings with posters of pictures of her favourite boy band, The Pagans.

But things did not work out too badly for the downtrodden Mr Ug. Quite often he could be seen walking Rover (what else?) down the track, and, after glancing over his shoulder, slipping into The Cave Inn. He, too, had set a pattern for generations of husbands to come!

IN SICKNESS AND IN HEALTH...

Paul Dufour, guide dog owner

I feel that Reilly has shown himself to be a very resourceful and adaptable guide dog for me. I qualified with him in June 2002. He had been out working before and had encountered problems, which had left him severely lacking in confidence. However, with careful handling and patience he successfully came back into work. This is when I came into his life.

I was just building up a bond with Reilly, after three months together, when I became ill and was taken into hospital to undergo major heart surgery. Reilly was rehomed back to his puppy walkers. He stayed with them for four months until I was able to start working with him again.

Four months after getting him back, I became a student at a residential college in Birmingham, and Reilly had to learn to adapt to a whole new environment and change of lifestyle. Two weeks into my course, I was taken back into hospital and Reilly had to cope with the loss of me, and get used to various different handlers from the residential and teaching staff. We soon picked up where we left off and started to work well together.

I have since had to undergo more hospital stays, and Reilly has had to cope yet again with my absences, and all the disruption that goes with them. Despite all the upheavals in his short working life, I think Reilly has shown himself to be a very reliable and resourceful, loving, working guide dog.

MISTY MISBEHAVING

Peter Storer,
former Sgt Warwickshire Police Dog Section.

It was an honour to be a Police Dog Handler with the Warwickshire Police for 16 years. Together with my partner Cyril Bloor, from Stratford-upon-Avon, I was chosen to train the first dual-trained explosives search dogs in the UK outside the Metropolitan Police. We attended the Home Office Police Dog School, then based in Stafford, for an initial course lasting eight weeks.

My dog was a three-year-old German Shepherd called Misty. The use of bitches as general purpose dogs was actually frowned on by most forces at that time, for no apparent reason apart from the fact that maybe it was not macho to work a lady dog! To get over the problem of seasons Misty was neutered, and through competing in many working trials she proved that she was more than capable of beating the lads. She was the best tracking/searching German Shepherd that I ever came across in my career.

Following our qualification at Stafford, Cyril and I worked our two dogs as a team at hundreds of different functions throughout the county where there was a potential threat to individuals, such as during royal visits, or to organisations. Our brief was to ensure that buildings and surrounding areas were free from any kind of improvised explosive devices and this, at times, could get a little hairy, as you can imagine (there lie many more stories for future books!).

One such story became a topic at the Association of Senior Police Officers Annual "jolly' during the speeches – and it also hit the national newspapers.

Misty and I were summoned to the then new Farmers Mutual Insurance Offices in Stratford, which were being opened by HRH Princess Anne. The building was comprised of brand new 'open plan' offices, which were the fad of the era. Each large office was furnished with new office equipment and the most wonderful plain beige carpet.

Misty started her search on the ground floor, and we worked our way up through all the floors. The rooms were very hot, and so I worked her in ten-minute intervals, with ten minutes' rest, so she did not tire and lose concentration. However, time began to run out before the arrival of HRH, so I pushed her a little harder. To my amazement, she suddenly just stopped work and refused to go on, staying rooted to the spot, staring up at me with those dark, angelic eyes. I asked her to go on – but nothing, she just stood there. This was not my Misty, she was a workaholic, so I tried to work out what the problem was. I did not have to wait long!

Misty suddenly squatted down and produced a big pile all over the lovely new beige carpet, right next to a rather aloof lady office worker. The lady leapt from her chair crying: "My God, Princess Anne is due here at any moment and I have been chosen to meet her here! What shall we do?" She promptly started to cry.

A lovely aroma started to rise from the steaming pile, which made her even worse. I tried to calm her down, but was interrupted by my radio announcing the arrival of the royal party. "Where is the cleaners'

Maybe HRH will think it's part of the pattern.

cupboard?" I asked frantically. I found it and retrieved the best I could find, which was a dustpan and brush. I cleaned up as well as I could, but it still left a large, brown stain on the carpet right next to the lady's desk.

"What shall we do?" she asked tearfully. "The Princess is due at any minute."

"Don't worry," I said, as cheerfully as possible. "She will never know," and I placed a large waste paper bin over the offending stain.

As I bailed out of the door at the other end of the room, HRH appeared at the other door to commence her visit and to be met by the unfortunate office worker – with smudged mascara – and the awful smell around her desk which was, by then, even more apparent.

I still wonder what HRH thought of her!

STAR STRUCK

Mike Mullan, dog trainer and
Kennel Club member

About four years ago a film company was making a film in Birmingham called Nasty Neighbours, which starred the very well-known character actor Ricky Tomlinson, and the equally famous actress Sheila Sims.

The film company wanted two dogs – a docile Yorkshire Terrier and an apparently aggressive Rottweiler – and I was asked to provide them. I got permission from some friends to use their Yorkshire

Terrier and, at the time, I owned a seven-year-old Rottweiler called Benjamin. Benjamin was a good working dog, who was trained to take the right arm on command, as police dogs do. However, the director wanted the dog to chase, attack and grab the rear end of a fleeing Ricky Tomlinson.

Initially I was given 21 days to prepare Benjamin for his film career, and suddenly 21 days were reduced to just 10 days. Given my normal heavy workload, could I prepare him in time? The answer had to be 'Yes', but it did leave a little doubt as to whether Benjamin would go for the arm or the backside on the day.

The day of filming dawned. We arrived in Birmingham on time and introduced Benjamin to his fellow actors.

To set the scene, Ricky Tomlinson played a door-to-door salesman who, on knocking on the door of a terraced house, was confronted by a surly owner and his equally aggressive dog.

After some verbal, abusive exchange, Benjamin would be required to chase Ricky down the garden path, out of the gate and down a 50 yard passage, getting closer and closer to him, snapping at his disappearing posterior.

The first take went quite well but, unfortunately, my voice commands to Benjamin from within the house were picked up by a microphone. The second take appeared good to me, but the director wanted more aggression from the dog so, before the third take, I wound Benjamin up and this really seemed to do the trick.

He flew down the path, chasing Ricky and really chomping at his posterior. The director said that it was exactly what he wanted – but he would like one more run to see if it could be improved upon.

To this suggestion Ricky immediately replied: "No way mate, that was too realistic!"

He then proceeded to remove from the back of his trousers the remains of a well-chewed-up newspaper and magazine.

SCRUMPTIOUS SCRUMPY

Mrs G. M Cox, guide dog puppy walker

Take:
1 cup of Retriever
1 cup of Labrador
2 Floppy Ears
1 cute pink nose
4 tbsp caramel colouring

then add

4 ozs of a loving nature
2 ozs of gentleness
a good pinch of kindness

Mix together with three cuddles a day and you have a puppy called Scrumpy – who will be dearly missed when he leaves us for his training.

MY DOG IS GOOD NEWS

Dennis Gill, guide dog owner

Taff is a Retriever/Labrador cross, and has been my guide for nine years. He is coming up to his 11th birthday, and is a wonderful guide, companion and friend, and always sensitive to my needs. On one occasion, whilst walking home, I collapsed in the street. Taff started to bark, which attracted attention, bringing out a neighbour who helped me home.

I work as a Guide Dogs branch chairman, speaker and fundraiser, and Taff has accompanied me on many occasions, visiting shows, etc. He is well known in the town, and has had his photo in the local paper numerous times.

QUIRK OF FATE

Erica Stratford, dog training club member

Fate took a hand on a dark, blustery Monday morning on 4th December 2002.

The dogs and I were returning from our normal early morning walk – through the fields near home, along the edge of the pond, heading towards the spinney. Twig, my rescue Belgian Shepherd bitch, was trotting ahead as normal, carefully avoiding the single strand electric fence which protects young saplings from marauding deer. Blizzard, my white German Shepherd, was walking just in front of me, carrying his mandatory log. Then, disaster struck.

A sudden gust of wind blew one of the plastic stakes, which supported the electric fence, out of the ground. The wire fell across Twiggy's back; she let out a shriek and bolted for the spinney. I yelled "Down!" Blizzard immediately stopped and dropped his log, but Twig had gone, vanished into the gloom. I hastily put Blizzard on his lead and set off in search of Twig, calling her name and whistling.

It seemed to take forever to reach the path through the trees, and when we reached the stile on the other side of the spinney – which leads on to the road where I park the car – there was still no sign of Twig. It was quite dark, but mercifully, at that time of the morning there is not much traffic.

We searched up and down the road, but as I couldn't see Twiggy anywhere, and there was no answer to my calls, I decided we had better go home in case, in her panic, she had made her way the quarter of a mile up the road to 'safety'.

She wasn't there!

I waited a while to see if she turned up, and then rang work to say I would be late. Leaving Blizzard in the garden so that if Twig turned up at home there would be a friendly face to greet her, I went out again. I drove slowly up and down the road, then parked the car where I usually leave it. I went back through the spinney and across the fields, whistling and calling Twig in case she was hiding. Still nothing, and I returned home feeling more and more desperate.

She wasn't there!

The postman and the dustmen came, and I asked them if they had seen Twig. They knew her quite well, because she loved everyone and would always wag her tail frantically, yap a greeting, and try to rush up to them for a pat. They were all concerned and agreed to keep an eye out for her. Then I rang the local vet, the police, the dog warden, the local radio station and the rescue centres, to report her missing. I also rang work again to say I was taking a day's holiday so I could continue my search.

The rest of the day was spent searching for an hour at a time, then returning home in case there was any news, going out again, sometimes on foot, sometimes in the car, and waiting for the phone to ring. I rang the neighbouring farmer, in case they had seen her, and asked them to keep a look out. At about one o'clock, the phone rang, but it was one of the girls from work asking if there was any news. That was the only call.

My searches continued, on foot through the woods and fields and in ever increasing circles in the car. Twig seemed to have vanished off the face of the earth.

The light was slowly beginning to fade, so I got Blizzard and set off to walk down the road again in a last desperate attempt to find her before it got too dark to see anything. There is a pavement on the opposite side of the road to the spinney; it goes down to a derelict transport cafe, which I had searched earlier. We walked down towards the cafe, stopped in a field gateway, and I got Blizzard to 'speak' in case Twig was hiding somewhere, and could hear her big, woolly friend.

There was no answer!

Finally, I crossed the road and we walked back along the grass verge towards the spinney. About 20 yards from the stile, Blizzard literally pulled me through a dense screen of undergrowth into the ditch. There lay poor dear Twiggy, in a heap, dead.

She was quite cold, and from the look of her injuries, she had been killed outright. I think she must have run out of the spinney, straight into a vehicle of some kind. But someone must have thrown her in the ditch, because there was no way she could have crawled there. Twiggy was wearing her collar with my name, address and phone number, and also a Dogs Trust lucky dog club scheme disc, so there was no excuse to leave her like that. I buried her in the spinney, where she loved to romp with her bestest pal, Blizzard, and chase the rabbits and squirrels.

The next week passed in a bit of a daze – no more would my little brown girl bounce over to greet me when I came home, she wouldn't be racing me when doing heelwork, and she wouldn't be doing her lightening recalls. But it wasn't until the following Saturday afternoon that I realised how much Blizzard was missing his soul mate.

We went for a walk, and he was plodding along like an old man. He wasn't picking up logs and prancing along showing them to me. He didn't even want to chase the cheeky squirrels in the wood – even when they flaunted themselves right under his nose. I had to do something to find him another friend.

On Sunday, we set off for the Dogs Trust kennels at Evesham, but I had forgotten they didn't open until one o'clock, so we took a detour to their kennels near Kenilworth. Unfortunately, most of their inmates were male, and that wouldn't have been very practical, because Blizzard likes to be 'in charge' where other males were concerned – another boy could have led to a few 'punch-ups' in the future.

Back we went to Evesham.

I explained what had happened (they already knew me, because I visited the kennels quite often before I got Twiggy).One of the girls said she thought they had something that might suit, but suggested I go and have a look around.

In the second block of kennels there was a young, almost black, collie bitch, with the biggest brown eyes you ever saw, almost popping out of her head. I looked round the other kennels, but was drawn back to the collie, in spite of the fact that I really didn't like the name on her run – 'Gertie'.

I went back to the office and asked if they would get her out, and three faces immediately lit up! "Are you trying to tell me something?" I asked. While Ian went to get her out, they explained that 'Gertie' (aka Dirty Gertie) had already had two homes. She had been taken to the kennels when she was just six months old, because the owners said she was destructive, and they couldn't house train her.

She was in the kennels for about three months when she was rehomed to a couple who they thought would be ideal. They had an older dog, and said they loved taking the dog for long, country walks. She lasted there for about another six months and then they brought her back. They said she was bullying their older dog!

I said: "She's got no chance of bullying Blizzard!" By then, Ian had arrived with a typically squirmy, excited collie, who wanted to leap all over me. As we walked up to the paddock, it became increasingly obvious that she had never had any lead training. She was nearly pulling Ian's arms out, and weaving from side to side in front of him – but then, I don't mind a challenge (I've got Blizzard). Ian kept saying: "She's ever so good off the lead!" trying to reassure me.

When we got to the paddock he let her off the lead, and threw a tennis ball. She raced after it, grabbed it in full flight, and then ran back to within about six yards of us, dropped it on the floor, lay down and crept backwards on her tummy, staring at it. I remarked: "She's got an awful lot of 'eye'!"

We then introduced her to Blizzard, in one of the runs. He did his usual form of greeting, by bouncing up to her going "Wow! Wow! Wow! (very off-putting to those who don't know him). She stood her ground, and when he got a bit boisterous, snapped at him. He immediately backed off, and as neither of them were 'nasty' about it, I decided that she could come and live with us, subject to a final vet check because she had banged her head in the kennel a couple of days before.

That night I sat at home trying to think what I

would call her, because I definitely didn't think 'Gertie' suited her. I almost called her 'Frog' because of her big bulging eyes, and the way she leaped about all the time. Then a name just popped into my head: 'Quirk!', 'Quirky!' 'Quirk of Fate' – because if it hadn't been for a quirk of fate, I would never have met her. A week later, she came home with us.

Well she's certainly Quirky, but that's another story . . .

GETTING A BUZZ FROM SNOWY

Jenny Moir, head of PR,
Hearing Dogs for Deaf People

Mongrels Snowy and her sister Sooty were young puppies in an RSPCA shelter until they were selected for training as hearing dogs. Both are now working hearing dogs, and since she has been with her profoundly deaf owner, Sarah O'Leary, Snowy has enjoyed a lovely life, with her sense of fun coming to the fore.

She loves working and telling Sarah about the sounds, but she does take it too far sometimes! On one occasion she came running to find Sarah and alerted her, then led her to the bathroom where she started jumping around the room. When Sarah looked closely she discovered that Snowy was drawing her attention to a fly!

Snowy also has a rather peculiar love of feet – and apparently the smellier the better. Whoever takes their socks off near her gets the Snowy treatment; she will lick their feet until the cows come home!

Look - it's a fly!

ON GUARD

Ian Weston, guide dog owner

On Thursday 27th November last year, I was travelling with my guide dog Voss on the train from Basingstoke to Reading. I was in the rear carriage, and after the announcement that we had arrived at Reading station (and with hindsight, erroneously told to alight the train), I made my way with Voss to the open doors.

I asked Voss to go forward, but he would not move and I wondered why. I repeated the command,

Mind the gap!!

and, again, he refused to respond. I felt bemused at Voss' refusal to comply, as my beloved, faithful, two-year-old guide dog was always so obedient. I asked Voss a third time, and with that he moved in front of me and pushed me backwards into the middle of the coach. It turned out that the tarin had stopped short of the platform, and Voss was ensuring my safe distance from the great drop on to the open track. Voss, my hero, had saved my life. A few seconds later a fast Intercity train went past – if Voss had obeyed my commands I cannot begin to think of the tragic consequences. Voss went beyond the call of duty and I will be eternally grateful to him for saving my life; he is my devoted friend and loving companion.

THAT'S THE SPIRIT...

Tom Buckley, British instructor of professional dog trainers

Having reached the stage in life when nature tells me that time is no longer on my side, I cannot help thinking of missed chances and experiences. As far as I am aware there have not been many, but, even so, I would not be averse to a visit from the Good Fairy with her menu of wishes.

The proverbial health, wealth and happiness are not what I am really looking for. I think I have more than my fair portion of all three. What I am really looking for are opportunities to solve life's enigmas, or the chance to open the 'Closed Book of Knowledge'.

Being able to see a ghost, or having an actual

conversation with some dogs would do for starters. I am totally frustrated from spending years talking to dogs, but being unable to understand their reasons for doing things. I would give nearly anything to hear them speak in a language that I could understand – not the sign language I have only guessed they are using.

Seeing a ghost is another matter altogether!

It all started when the late Ron Darbyshire and I owned a security company that specialised in the use of dogs. In the early days, we both had to do guarding shifts when we were short of handlers for one reason or another. Our clients covered a number of industries, but the most unusual of these was an iron foundry situated in North Manchester. If you have ever wondered where those three-legged cooking pots – the sort that feature in cartoons depicting cannibals and explorers – were made, look no further.

Being a foundry, black sand from the moulds seemed to get everywhere. Needless to say, it was not a popular assignment with our handlers, and was made even less so with rumours of the occasional sighting of an apparition, thought to be one of the original owners of the company. Tales of apprentices running and screaming out of the building, and even a foreman appearing ashen-faced and shaking, did not help.

During one particularly busy period when we were stretched for relief guards, Ron volunteered to do a couple of night duties at the foundry. The morning after his first shift, he telephoned me. His side of the conversation went something like this: "I am never going near that place again, even if it means losing the contract. I will do anyone else's shift elsewhere but, as far as I am concerned, there are some things I will not subject my dog to".

If I remember rightly, his dog at the time was Parro of Charavigne, a former Swedish Army Dog of a far from delicate nature! I naturally tried to find out more, but Ron just said that he was sorry for the inconvenience he was causing, but he did not wish to discuss it now – or ever.

A few months passed, and it came to my turn to step into the breech… guess where? The foundry, of course. I had not forgotten the Ron incident, but I did not give the ghost thing a second thought. Why, you might ask. Easy, I just did not believe in them.

Nothing untoward happened that night, or on two other occasions around that period. The fourth night was somewhat different.

Although we used a weighbridge office between our rounds of the premises, because of the all-pervading black sand we ate our meals in an adjacent general office. This was a long, rectangular room, with windows on the right-hand side looking out to a side street. The left side was the blank wall dividing it from the main factory. Along the bottom of the room, a wood and glass partition had been constructed which acted as a corridor leading from the side street door to the factory. The timber was waist height, with glass above, so that it was possible to see anyone walking along the corridor. Halfway along was a door, fitted with a Yale-style lock and an automatic 'door closer'.

I would sit on a high stool with my dog lying on the floor where he really could not have had much of a view. The area had its own electric light, and two or three lights were always left on in the main room. The corridor was also lit.

It was about 4am and, after returning from a

patrol, I was having my last cup of tea of the shift while browsing through a book. Whether I had nodded off for a moment or two, I am not sure, but I became aware of a vibration from under the desk. It was a belly growl coming from Warden, my dog – a growl you could feel rather than hear. He was now standing facing down the room, towards the corridor. His hackles were standing up like bristles on a yard brush. I looked in the direction he was pointing to see the central door open almost fully, and then slowly close, controlled by the pneumatic closer.

When I think about it now, I still have an uneasy feeling. At the time, it took several minutes for Warden and I to pull ourselves together and to go and examine the outside door, which turned out to be securely locked. Needless to say, the incident was not recorded in any report book, and it was many months before I even mentioned it at home.

Why would any supernatural spirit need to open a door? Surely it could walk straight through it? Perhaps it opened through air pressure caused by strong winds – but not that night, which was particularly still. Could it be something to do with the door closer developing a fault, which caused it to work in reverse? I think that would be too far-fetched.

The only other practical theory is that a work's employee knew how to get in and had hidden himself in order to play a practical joke.

By crawling on hands and knees from the factory end of the corridor, he would have been hidden from view by the waist-high partition.

He could have pushed the door open slowly, and nipped back before it closed. However, knowing the reputation of our dogs, it would have taken a very courageous or foolhardy person to undertake such a pointless and stupid act. Also, it was 4 am.

Some 20 years after this event, I told Ron the story of that night and asked him if his experience had been similar. All he would say was: "It had been something like that". I did not press the matter, as I could see he was not at all comfortable and wished to forget it.

If only Warden could have told me what sounds, scents, temperature changes, or whatever, had caused him to react in such a way.

In case you are thinking that I have not ever mentioned the customary third wish – I have decided to give it a miss. Finding out what is beyond mortality will come soon enough!

SEASON OF ALARM

A tale of the late Derek Freeman (for 27 years Guide Dogs' breeding manager)

Derek Freeman was not renowned for his timekeeping. This was due largely to the fact that he was so interested in his job, and loved talking to people, so that the hours would slip by without him noticing.

Towards the end of his career he received a richly deserved MBE. Parking his car in a designated park near to Buckingham Palace, he duly went in and accepted his 'gong'. As usual, he was the last to leave as he was probably enthralling the Royal Family with lurid tales from the mating shed. Inevitably, his was

the last car to remain in the park and, on his return, he found it was being investigated by the Metropolitan Police, as a 'sniffer' dog had taken a very keen interest in it and had actually indicated a possible bomb.

Just before the car was blown skywards, Derek was able to solve the mystery.

"I revealed all and told them the truth. The previous day I had had a couple of bitches in the car, which were in full season. Your dog is less interested in finding a bomb than in having his wicked way!"

POLE POSITION

Norman McIver, guide dog instructor

I used to be a Royal Air Force dog handler. One day I competed in the Station Trials at RAF Leuchars. The exercise involved walking the dog to heel off the lead, getting him to sit before negotiating an obstacle, and then back to heel. Well, I was on a clear round with just the 'sendaway' to do (which involves pointing the dog towards a distant object and getting him to run to it).

I was very confident that my dog Rhani would easily cover at least 75 yards in a straight line. I gave him the command to go, and he set off like a bullet. However, after about 15 yards he did a 90 degree turn and proceeded for about 50 yards where he found one of the jumps. He then lay down and watched proceedings from his new found den.

After my initial embarrassment I did find this very funny!

A REASSURING NOISE

Norman McIver, guide dog instructor

A few years ago I trained a lady from Dundee. It was her first guide dog, and after a couple of weeks she said she was very upset, because she felt the dog had not formed any attachment to her and was still looking for me, her old trainer. The dog was actually working well for her, so I reassured her that there really was not a problem. However, I was not going to be able to change her opinion easily.

A few days later, I saw a big difference. The lady reported that the dog had let out a plaintive 'squeal' when she had left her in a room, and this showed that she was now attached. This happened again, but the lady then discovered it was the door squeaking as it closed! However, the problem was solved.

LONG WAY HOME

Chris Wade, guide dog owner

On Wednesday 28th January 2004, due to severe snow, rain and ice causing major traffic gridlock, my journey home from work was extremely difficult.

I eventually managed to catch a train from Coventry to Rugby, and on my arrival in Rugby I realised that the only way to get home was to walk.

The journey home from the railway station is approximately four miles, and the pavements were very icy. I eventually got home safely at 9.15 pm having left work at 4.45 pm – thanks, of course, to Victor.

Cheer up Chris – only four miles to go!

IN THE LINE OF DUTY

Neil Ewart, author

Ivor, a yellow Labrador, worked with a piano tuner in Hertfordshire during the 1970s. His owner, Harold, had been blind since birth. He was always very active and had decided to apply for his first guide dog in 1970. He trained at Leamington Spa.

Ivor had been bred by The Guide Dogs For The Blind Association, and puppy walked in Birmingham for the first 12 months of his life. I have very fond memories of him as Ivor was the first guide dog I ever trained. An extremely mature dog at a relatively early age, he flew through his training having the ability and willingness to learn his tasks very quickly. After one month's training with Ivor, Harold returned home to his piano tuning job, which involved travelling all over the county, visiting different homes every working day.

One dark evening, Ivor was guiding Harold along a narrow footpath running alongside the main railway line from London to Scotland. Suddenly, the dog stopped and would not proceed. Despite cajoling, he still refused. Eventually a member of the public came from the same direction and was asked if there was an obvious explanation for the dog's reticence. At first he could not see anything, but as he walked on contact was made with a transparent fishing line, which, presumably, youths had stretched across the footpath to ambush the unwary.

The remarkable point of this true story is that Ivor had stopped well before the line without making any

contact . Also, it was nearly dark. So, the question is, how did he know?

On a lighter note, a similar incident occurred a couple of years later for very different reasons. While holidaying in Norfolk, Ivor and Harold set off to explore some country lanes.

At a certain point, Ivor stopped and refused to proceed further. Harold turned back for a short distance, then tried again. Still Ivor came to a full stop.

Hearing agitated voices behind him he asked for the reason. "Ah well," came a broad Norfolk brogue, "our bull's got loose in the lane and he and the dog have been face to face. We don't know which is the more surprised to see the other".

RICKY: READY FOR ANYTHING

Iris Cooksley, guide dog owner

Ricky became my guide dog on November 1st, 1997. A week later roadworks started – a by-pass for Billingshurst, and building galore ever since. There's no knowing where to cross the road, but Ricky notices even the tiniest obstacle.

I count on his steadfastness tackling Cumbrian Fells, bustling seaside resorts, the theatre or train journeys across London.

My busy social life sees him stretching out at yoga, blessed at the communion rail, raising an eyebrow at hairdresser's chatter, and bringing joy to a housebound couple. Ricky truly is my other half.

PERPETUAL MOTION

Ian Armstrong, guide dog instructor

Many years ago we accepted a lot of adult dogs from the public for training as guide dogs. All would go through a fairly rigorous assessment before entering formal training.

I remember following a young lady trainer with a Labrador who had been with us for a couple of weeks. He was actually showing very good potential, and we took him into Leamington to see his reactions to unusual obstacles. At that time, the town

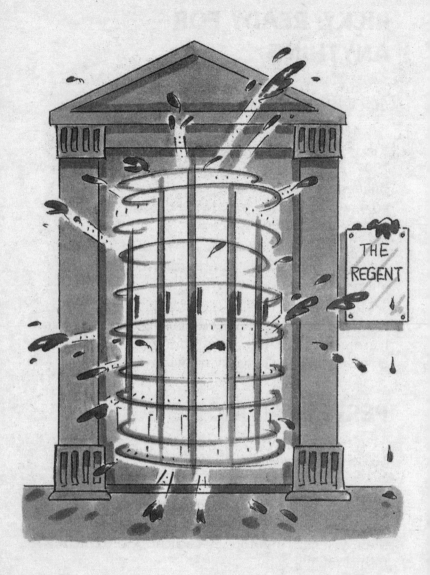

centre boasted a rather nice hotel called The Regent, and the entrance consisted of revolving doors. The handler took the dog up to the entrance, and proceeded to go through, with the intention of quickly visiting the foyer and coming straight out again. This was common practice, and the hotel would always welcome us.

All went well, and the doors had nearly completed one hundred and eighty degrees when the dog suddenly, and without warning, squatted producing a rather large pile. Extricating herself and the dog, the handler beckoned to me to follow her in and hold the dog while she cleared up the mess. Unfortunately, at that moment a gentleman hurtled past me, setting the revolving door off like a catherine wheel!

The resultant mess and embarrassment all round I will leave to your imagination.

OUT OF THE FRYING PAN...

Dany Grosemans, Belgian pet behaviour counsellor and founder of the Belgian centre for guide dogs

I was asked to visit a family with a male Golden Retriever, 18 months old. The dog had 'threatened' the mother and the two daughters of the family on a number of occasions.

When I arrived, I was shown into the living room by the female members of the family. The man of the house was watching television, and looked as if he was nothing to do with the problem – and certainly had no interest in solving it.

I spent about 10 minutes discussing the dog's behaviour with the mother and her daughters (aged 25 and 26 years respectively), and then the man came to the table. He immediately interrupted the conversation and told me: "You know what? I'll tell you what the problem is! They (pointing to the three women) have spoiled the dog!"

He went on to tell me of a situation that, he claimed, proved his point.

A few days earlier, there had been a football game on television. Being a big football fan he liked his family to leave him alone in the house while he was watching a match. He told me that about five minutes after the match had started, the dog began to make funny noises. He asked the dog if he wanted to go out. The dog looked towards the back door, and the man had to leave his football game to let the dog out in the garden. But within a few minutes, the dog was whining to be let back in again.

Back inside the house, the dog refused to let the man enjoy his football, and continued to yelp and to whine.

"I know they" – he said, pointing at the women – "give him treats sometimes. The dog was staring at the kitchen door, so I went and got him a biscuit. But you know what? The biscuit had no effect at all. I asked him if he wanted another biscuit, then a third biscuit. But the dog refused to calm down. His eyes were fixed on the kitchen counter where there was a bowl of pancake mix. Can you imagine, sir, that the only way to satisfy him was baking a pancake for him? Only after he got his pancake would he leave me alone to watch my football game."

When the man stopped talking, I watched for the reaction of the women. They all looked guilty and upset by the man's story.

I looked at the man and said: "OK, who spoils this

dog?" I waited a split second, and, just before he could answer, I asked him:

"Who baked the pancake for the dog?"

GUARDIAN ANGEL

Jenny Moir, head of PR,
Hearing Dogs for Deaf People

Valentine is an amazing mongrel. Not only is she a working hearing dog for her profoundly deaf owner, June Beech, but she is a life-saver, paramedic and guardian angel.

Being deaf, June cannot hear household sounds like the doorbell, telephone, alarm clock and smoke alarm. However, she never misses any of these because Valentine is there to let her know by touching her with a paw and leading June to whatever it is – except when the alarm sounds when she knows to drop to the floor to indicate danger. Valentine was trained to use this 'touch and tell' method of alerting to sounds, and she has used it on many occasions to avert possible tragedies.

The first time was when June's father-in-law was staying with them. He was having a lie-in in bed, while June was doing some gardening. Unbeknown to June, he suddenly had a stroke and fell out of bed. Although he was unable to cry for help, which June would not have heard anyway, fortunately Valentine had heard the sound of him falling and rushed into the bedroom to investigate. She quickly realised that she needed to get June, so ran to find her at the bottom of the garden. She touched June with her paw, then led her back up to the bedroom, where June found her father-in-law collapsed on the floor. He was rushed to hospital, and luckily recovered – thanks to Valentine's swift actions.

A little while after that incident, Valentine was taken ill with viral enteritis and very nearly lost her life. She came through it, and was allowed home to recover, but June was advised that she should try not to let Valentine work for a little while. However, Valentine had other ideas – fortunately for June and her husband Steve. During this convalescent period, while June was in the kitchen preparing dinner, Steve had gone out into the garage, closing the patio doors after him as it was raining very heavily.

A few minutes later, Valentine jumped up from her bed where she was resting, and started alerting June with her paw. June assumed she was after some titbits, so told her to go back to bed, which she did. But a few seconds later, she rushed into the kitchen and flung herself at June, frantically touching her with her paw. June realised that something was dreadfully wrong, and followed Valentine, who took her to the patio doors.

With a shock, June saw that Steve had collapsed on the patio and was lying unconscious in the pouring rain. He was rushed to hospital with a suspected brain haemorrhage, but thankfully made a full recovery. If Valentine had not realised that something was wrong, he could have lain outside unnoticed by June for quite a long time, and probably would not have survived.

But Valentine's heroic deeds do not stop there. She was out walking in town with June one day, and June decided to cross the busy road. Rather than make her way to a pedestrian crossing, June opted to cross the road between two parked lorries. She checked both ways then started to walk across the road. Valentine, however, would not move and kept backing towards the pavement. June tried to coax her, but Valentine just refused.All of a sudden, June looked up and saw a huge lorry passing close by and travelling quite fast. June had not seen it, or obviously heard it, coming and she then realised that if Valentine had not refused to move, they would both have been hit and possibly killed by the lorry. Once again, Valentine had acted above and beyond the call of duty.

Soon after that incident, on a separate occasion when June was standing waiting to cross a road, Valentine moved in front of her and lay down, to stop her stepping out when the coast was not clear.

Valentine has the most amazing capacity for caring, not only for her beloved owner, but for everyone she meets. June's grandson was on the receiving end of Valentine's loving nature when he was a toddler. He was playing out in the garden on a windy day, when a sudden gust blew him into a bush where he cut himself quite badly. Even before he had time to start crying, Valentine had reached his side and was comforting him, and stayed close to him all day.

Little wonder then that June really does believe that Valentine is her guardian angel.

ON TAP

Bill Logan, guide dog instructor

When we trained guide dog owners at residential centres, the dogs would usually be issued on the second or third day. After issuing the first dog and leaving the new owner in his bedroom with the dog so they could get to know each other, I made my way down the corridor to give out another two. As I dropped off the third, the first guy popped his head out of his bedroom door and asked if I could come and look for his dog as it had gone missing.

I rushed back to his room and looked in. The dog was there – but for reasons known only to itself it was sitting in the sink!

SITTING TIGHT

Norman McIver, guide dog instructor

There is an old but true story about a dog working in Dumfermline who refused to cross a road. The guide dog owner could not hear any traffic and became more insistent, but still the dog would not go forward. Then he heard a voice saying: "Thanks mate," and discovered the dog was waiting for two people to push a broken-down car up the street.

A DOG OF MY OWN

Nick Mays, Chief Reporter, Our Dogs

As I mentioned before, I didn't actually have a dog of my own until I was 26 years old. Marianne, my wife (now ex, then new) was a seasoned dog owner – she had owned a dog since she was about 13 years old, the lucky thing. But as she had moved from Sweden to England to marry me, she had to leave her elderly Golden Retriever, Jesper (that's Swedish for Jasper) over there with her Mum, as she didn't want to subject him to six months' quarantine. (No Pet Passports in those days).

In order to keep her happy I had agreed to our getting a dog at the earliest opportunity. Well, it wasn't too much hardship for me – I had wanted a dog for years. Thus it was that, a few days after we moved into our new house, we bought a blue roan Cocker Spaniel puppy named Bonnie. We didn't even have a bed or a washing machine or curtains for our front room – all that sort of thing was in hand for later. The dog came first!

Bonnie proved to be a very individualistic puppy with some very definite ideas about how things should be – i.e. they should be her way! Of course, in time, we trained her to an acceptable standard of behaviour, but until then, I had to get used to such doggy foibles as leaving me a 'present' on the bedroom floor so when I lurched up off the sun lounger I'd been sleeping on (still no bed remember) I'd get a wet, warm feeling under my bare feet (and a ripe smell to go with it). Since then, I've always made sure my carpet slippers are worn around the house, and I take care to look inside them before putting them on first thing of a morning – because carpet slippers themselves aren't immune to being ideal places for a puppy to deposit a present.

Nice though Bonnie was – I've seen dogs with entire tails that couldn't wag them as fast as she could wag her docked stump – Marianne was still missing her Jesper, so after a few months, we tracked down the top breeder of Golden Retrievers in the country and made a long car journey to pick up a puppy who would, in fact, be related to Jesper. Of course, Bonnie came along for the ride, as she went everywhere with us. But she stayed in the car while we selected our puppy out of the roly-poly, yellow butterballs of fur at the breeder's home. When we chose our puppy – a handsome, grinning lad, named Leo – he sat with Marianne on the back seat next to Bonnie. Leo snuffled a greeting to the floppy-eared dark dog opposite. Bonnie responded with a growl that clearly said: "Don't forget who's in charge, Sonny!"

Leo never forgot this, even when he grew a lot bigger than Bonnie. Nice though Goldens are, they aren't over-blessed in the brainbox department, and Leo was no exception – whereas Bonnie had brains in abundance, and a devious nature to go with them. If she wanted something done, she would get Leo to do it for her – and he would do it gladly, with a big soppy grin on his face. A classic example of this was the time she made him knock all my houseplants down off the living room windowsill. She then gave them a good shaking to get rid of all the earth before she ate them. (I was a novice dog owner – houseplants with young dogs around? Forget it!)

Or there was the time that we went Christmas shopping. We left the two of them – both still relative youngsters – in the kitchen, a child-gate keeping them in place. We asked two friends to come in during the day, let them out into the garden for a wee, and see that all was well. When we came home, we were surprised by the amount of dust on the kitchen table, work surfaces and just about everywhere else in the kitchen... and the fact that a full bag of cat litter was now empty. According to our friends, they had come in to find Leo proudly holding the empty cat litter bag in his mouth, cat litter all over the kitchen floor. He had obviously dragged the sack around, spilling its contents, and distributing them nice and evenly over as wide an area as possible. Not only that, but our three cats, delighted at having found an extended litter tray had decided to use it as much as possible.

It was quite clear who had been behind Operation Cat Litter – Bonnie could never mask her feelings. Like my old Boxer pal Buster, she would show the whites of her eyes and look incredibly shifty. In fact, it was very easy to visualise her saying to Leo; "Look Leo – see that cat litter sack over there? I want it. Bring it here!" And Leo responded: "Duh! Okay Bonnie! Shall I drag it all over the floor for you, too?"

"Why not?" she'd say, "What larks!"

Mind you, much as Leo was put upon by Bonnie, he forgot his place in the pecking order whenever they went for a walk – especially on cold, wet winter days when she was wearing her waterproof coat. Leo's favourite trick was to bowl her over and try and pull her coat off, usually leaving with it pulled inside out over her eyes. As soon as we sorted her out and straightened her coat, she would fly at Leo – literally fly through the air – teeth bared. It was all good fun really – Leo would allow her to maul him about a bit, then give chase. Bonnie being small and fast could make tight turns, which Leo, being big and gangly and, later, big and heavy, couldn't do. He would skid in the mud and end up in a pile of legs, covered with mud, looking more like a Flatcoat Retriever than a Golden Retriever!

Looking back, I think Leo had an identity crisis for a while because he would run up to every Cocker Spaniel he saw, thinking they were kinsfolk – and very often getting barked at for his trouble. In fact, I'm sure it was Bonnie who told him one day that he was a Golden Retriever, and this prompted him to snaffle Marianne's jewellery box and eat all her gold jewellery! Yes, it did go through him and come out the other end, but alas, not intact. It had been well chewed beforehand!

Sadly, the indomitable team was broken up when Bonnie had to be put to sleep at four years old with a brain tumour, but Leo had company by then in the form of fellow Golden and relative Jesper. Yes, he was imported from Sweden after all. He had been so miserable without Marianne that it was agreed that he should come and live here. Luckily, we were able to select a very good quarantine kennels not too far from where we lived, and Marianne made great efforts to see him every day for the first few weeks of his stay, then at least three times a week thereafter, allowing him to get settled. Six months passed by quickly and soon he was home with us. He deferred to Leo after one small spat over who was in charge and spent many happy years with us, finally passing away at the grand old age of 11, which was very good, considering his various aches and pains.

We kept many dogs over the years, including a number of elderly rescues. The sad thing with a 'golden oldie' is that you know they will not be with you for very long, but they can be a delight while they are. There was Sheba, the Golden Retriever/Rough Collie cross who used the attributes of both breeds to great effect. There was the total adoration and affection of the Golden, coupled with the sharp intelligence (and snout) of the Rough Collie. If you were reading a newspaper and not showing Sheba the attention she craved, invariably a long Collie nose would 'beak' up through the newspaper. Similarly, if breakfast wasn't forthcoming fast enough in the morning, she would use her beak to attract your attention. And on a winter's morning, a cold wet nose on the end of a long Collie snout going up your dressing gown with force certainly wakes you up, take it from me!

Then there was Rufus, the Cavalier King Charles Spaniel who headed an unholy trinity of 'Cavvies' in later years. A very happy-go-lucky little dog, he found a big buddy in Leo, who would gently and patiently play 'tug' with his little friend, allowing Rufus to win the tugging rope more often than not. And with a name like Leo, well – why not play lions too? Rufus's party piece was to put his head in Leo's mouth like a brave lion tamer – with never an accident either!

When he was older, Rufus became a very handsome little dog. Our Golden Retriever bitch Elsa certainly thought so, spurning the advances of Leo's successor and nephew Dandy, and, instead, playing up to Rufus! Needless to say, rakish Rufus took it all in his stride and would have been quite prepared to give Elsa his full attention (she even crouched down low for him!) if only we'd have let him.

When our eldest daughter Rebecca was a toddler, Rufus was her bestest buddy in the whole world – even when in his exuberance at chasing her and jumping up at her, he pulled her trousers down one day! When she was a little older, she chose to have her face painted like Rufus at an exemption dog show and then promptly went into the ring with Rufus to win the Dog and Owner Look-alike class. I think Rufus must have been quite an influence on her behaviour – and on her imagination, too. One day when I took her to nursery, her teacher said: "Hello Rebecca. Are you going to be Doggy Rebecca today?" On another occasion I came to collect her from nursery and all the children ran out barking! I think someone had been influencing them...

Nowadays, I own a very lazy Golden named Emma, a positively calm dog when compared to some of her predecessors. But she suddenly comes to life when she sees her friend Tag, the German Shepherd, who lives nearby. Then, she becomes rather coquettish, she flutters her eyelashes (and she's got long eyelashes too!), and then she leads Tag a merry dance. I have always thought that there's a lot more going on with dogs then we humans suspect.

One thing's for sure though… it may have taken me years to have a dog of my own, but I'd never be without one now!

MAGIC WANDA

Mhairi Thurston, guide dog owner

Wanda has proved herself to be exceptional. I have three small children, aged 7, 6 and 3, which means that Wanda needs to be very adaptable. Every day Wanda leads the children and I to school down country lanes, with many stops and starts to empty stones from three pairs of shoes, sort out varying degrees of squabbles, and look at things along the way. She then runs the playground gauntlet while we deliver the youngest child to nursery. There are bells ringing, and there is noise and chaos everywhere.

While the children are at school Wanda often guides me on to the bus and into the busy town centre to do shopping. When we pick up the children again, Wanda takes us to our after-school activities (this is where she really shines). She goes with us to ballet, tap-dancing, gymnastics, swimming lessons and horse riding, not forgetting choral union on Monday nights.

She patiently endures a life surrounded by noise

and children. Sometimes when our youngest is doing yet another Hokey Cokey, with Wanda's "left paw in", I'm thankful that she is so very patient, loyal and adaptable. Having Wanda has transformed all of our lives – she is adored wherever we go.

There's no business like show business.....

SUMMING UP

Guide dog puppy walkers

Raising a guide dog puppy for the first year of its life can be rewarding and demanding in equal measure. Here, Guide Dogs puppy walkers recall some of their most memorable moments.

Aden: *"Right then, lets clean this up."*
Labrador Aden was very hyperactive – ripping, tearing and digging were his pastimes. We used to stand looking at his path of destruction wondering what he would do next.

Scrumpy: *"Wipe your mouth please."*
Scrumpy, super pup, who we are currently walking, is five months old. He's such a messy drinker and leaves a trail of water all over the kitchen floor, then puts his paws in the wet as he doubles back to get another drink – you just can't win can you?

Dee: *"What shall we talk about today?"*
Gentle, serene Dee used to sit outside our bedroom door every morning while I was drying my hair. I used to chat away to her about girlie things as if she knew what I was talking about.

Karl: *"Pardon you."*
Gentle giant Karl had a problem with wind and could clear a room in 30 seconds, need I say any more?

Shane: *"What have you got in your mouth now?"*

Shane was affectionate and funny, but had to try everything in his mouth. He used to look at me, his mouth swollen with rubbish, trying not to chew it. It was my duty to dispose of these mucky items. That year the bill for hand wash and cream doubled.

Sadler: *"People don't want you jumping up."*

Poser Sadler was a jumper, so when people came close to him Barry used to keep him under control, gently talking to him and uttering those immortal words.

Daniel: *"Off to bed are we?"*

Daniel was the calm, loyal pup but he was also a creature of habit. At 8pm every evening he would raise himself from a nap, have a good stretch, look at Barry for permission and pad off to bed. He must have found us boring!

Earl: *"I have just Hoovered there."*

Handsome Earl had perfect timing. He was secured out of the way while I Hoovered the house, and the first thing he would do when he was allowed back – yes, you've guessed it – give himself a good shake.

Jenks: *"Leave those flowers alone."*

Jenks was a free spirit, and he had a love of flower heads. My voice used to bellow down the garden, especially when he got too near to my Cliff Richard rose.

TOP DOGS

Richard Foster, guide dog owner

I have chosen four incidents concerning three of my guide dogs. Holley and Umber were yellow Labradors, and Digby is a black Labrador. Umber and Digby were bred by Guide Dogs; Holley was donated by a member of the public.

I confess to a tear as I write about Umber, who was recently put to sleep at the grand age of 14, having lost the use of his back legs. I do not claim he was the best worker ever, but he was more than adequate, and a lovely sensitive chap – just right for me!

Mind Reader

For two years in the mid-1970s, I taught in London for two days a week. Holley, a truly remarkable guide dog, would, when it came to going home in the evening, emerge from the Underground line at Victoria, then pause for a second while she looked to find the most convenient route to the platform on the main line that I needed.

Then, swiftly and efficiently, she would guide me to a free space on a bench nearest to where I needed to be to catch the train home.

On one occasion, it being the end of term, we finished an hour earlier than usual. At this time, the appropriate train home left from a different platform. As we walked along I thought: 'We need to go to a different platform. I wonder if, by any chance, Holley will realise?'

We seemed to turn off slightly earlier and she located a free bench. I heard some footsteps and I enquired whether I was at the correct platform. Remarkably, I was!

At the start of the next term we finished work at the usual time, and Holley took me, without hesitation, to the normal platform.

I cannot explain what prompted her to deviate on that day – but she certainly seemed to know what she was doing...

Plum Greedy

I was spending a few days with a friend. One morning Holley went for her usual inspection of the garden and, feeling a bit hungry, as Labradors often are, she was seen to pick up a plum. She then managed to remove the stone and promptly ate the fruit. This was obviously not enough for her, so she then proceed to crack open the stone and then ate the nut inside! You are probably asking yourself: "Was Holley sick?" I am happy to report that she was not.

Quick Thinking

I was walking along with Umber one day, with the main road on our left.

As we started to cross an entrance to a local gym, a vehicle suddenly turned into the drive.

Umber seemed to realise this would happen before it actually did, and he came to a sudden and definite stop.

I stepped back a pace, dropped the harness handle, and brought Umber to heel using the lead. The vehicle very swiftly pulled in without stopping. To this day,

I am convinced my guide dog saved me from serious injury, or, quite possibly, something even worse!

How he knew that the car was going to pull in front of us, before it actually did, is something I will never know.

This Takes the Biscuit

One day, I was in a shop with Digby. While I was being served, I removed his harness to make him more comfortable.

Being totally blind, I was unable to see what happened next – but was grateful to be told about it.

A lady spoke to me and said: "Your dog is absolutely remarkable.

"My little boy waved a partially eaten biscuit right in front of his nose, and he did not attempt to take it!"

Digby is my current guide dog. He really is too good for this world – something which, I regret, cannot be said of his master!

SCENTED AIR

Dany Grosemans,
Belgian pet behaviour counsellor and founder of the
Belgian centre for guide dogs

A client who had problems walking with his Borzoi in busy streets asked me to help him. At our first meeting, I told him how he should walk his dog and how to calm the dog when he became nervous of the passing cars, people, etc.

On my second visit, the man told me the dog had made major improvements, and so we decided to do a walk in the town centre.

When we passed a perfumery, the client told me that the owners of the shop had stopped him a few days earlier, and talked to him. He said we had better go into the shop so he could introduce me, as these people wanted to book an appointment with me.

We went into the shop. The owners immediately recognised my client, and I saw the woman signaling to her son. This young man opened a door, and out came a big, young, boisterous, male Dalmatian. Before anybody could get hold of him, he jumped on the Borzoi, who was terrified by this Dalmatian-style greeting. The Borzoi made himself small, and crawled to his owner.

I grabbed the Dalmatian by his collar, told the woman that it was not a good idea to let her dog do this; it was not at all necessary, and it would make her problem worse.

I gave the dog back to the son, and gave my visiting card to the woman.

I told her I couldn't do anything straight away, but she could phone me to make an appointment. All the time, I was dimly aware of a smell – other than perfume – pervading the shop. Then, I turned to my client, who had control of his dog again, and asked him to continue our walk outside.

When we left the shop I saw the origin of the strange smell. From the corner of my eye, I saw the marks of the Borzoi's anal glands that were left on the beautiful, red carpet.

When I visited the shop a week later to solve the problem with their Dalmatian, there were no marks left, and I didn't dare to ask. But I am sure it would have cost them lots of effort (and, probably, lots of money) to clean the carpet.

FRIENDLY RIVALRY

Norman McIver, guide dog instructor

Zing was the first guide dog I ever trained, and he went to Sam, who was a Rangers supporter. I am a Celtic supporter, and I remember during the first week of the training course we had a talk, then adjourned to a bar. Sam asked me to hold his dog while he went to the toilet. Despite only having been together for a matter of hours, the dog never took its eyes off the door and was delighted to see Sam come back. I had to admit that, despite supporting Rangers, he could still handle a dog!

Sam had a very big family, and twenty-two of them turned up for a meal. All went over to the pub, prior to sitting down to eat. However, they did not shut the kitchen door properly and Zing helped himself to twenty-two portions of chicken salad, thank you very much! Fortunately, there were no after-effects.

HOME FROM HOME

Patricia Rescigno, guide dog owner

My second guide dog, Isabel, is amazing. We have become a camping family and, upon arriving at the campsite, after setting up, Isabel and I head for the loo to check it out. My husband gives us directions to the loo, but when we return to the motor home I ask Isabel to: "find the motor home".

No matter where we are parked, how far away, how many distractions, Isabel always leads me right to the motor home door. She has become a proper little camper; she is very special.

I'd recognise a '95 Sundowner anywhere.

CAT COMFORTER

Jenny Moir, head of PR,
Hearing Dogs for Deaf People

Beautiful brindle mongrel Gypsy started her life as a stray and was rescued by the RSPCA. From there she was selected to train as a hearing dog, and has now been with her profoundly deaf owner, Janet Durbidge, for two years.

Despite a few traumas – being attacked by a large dog among them – she is a caring and loving little girl, who has made such a huge difference not only to Janet's life, but to that of Janet's elderly dog, Charlie. Before Gypsy arrived on the scene, Charlie was looking every one of his 13 years, and was suffering from fits and breathing attacks. However, the minute Gypsy arrived on the scene, she transformed Charlie and he took on a new lease of life. They became the best of friends, and Gypsy has taken on the role of caring for Charlie, particularly when it comes to thunderstorms, of which Charlie is terrified.

One afternoon when Janet was engrossed in reading in the living room, Gypsy came to her and touched her with her paw, then led Janet first to the French windows to show her that there was a hailstorm, then to Charlie, who was in his basket shaking with fear. Gypsy had worked out what was upsetting Charlie, and told Janet so that she could do something about it.

On another occasion, both dogs were out walking with Janet, who was throwing balls for them to chase. Charlie went off after the ball in one direction and ran out of sight, while Gypsy went off in another direction. Gypsy suddenly stopped mid-run, turned round and ran back to find Charlie. Janet followed her to see what was up, and found that Charlie was in agony having ruptured his cruciate ligament. By the time Janet got to him, Gypsy was already licking Charlie to soothe him, and she accompanied Janet and Charlie to the vet, comforting both dog and human alike.

Not only is Gypsy a carer, but she is a keen wildlife expert too. She has opened Janet's eyes to the world of nature, which she had not taken much notice of before.

One time Janet was sitting on a park bench with Gypsy beside her. Her ears kept flicking, and she kept looking in the direction of undergrowth on the other side of the pond.

Janet followed Gypsy's gaze to see what was so interesting, and suddenly she spotted a kingfisher. Without Gypsy's help, Janet would not have seen it at all. Gypsy has also helped Janet to spot frogs, squirrels and hedgehogs, which she could not hear.

So, whether it be as Florence Nightingale or David Attenborough – Gypsy fits the bill!

LONG DISTANCE DOGS

Ivan Pitchford, guide dog owner

During the last 10 years as a guide dog owner, I have become an avid long distance walker, John O'Groats

to Lands End being one of many such treks. My faithful guide dog and companion Helga has walked many a mile with me. Helga retired last year.

Luckily, Guide Dogs has done a fantastic job in matching me with my replacement dog, Fran. I decided to walk the length of Hadrian's Wall coast to coast (84 miles). This walk has been opened by the National Trust, with very well marked paths. Fran did a wonderful job of being a guide and companion while on this hazardous trek, and was a model of good behaviour during our overnight stops in various B&Bs. It goes without saying that I had a sighted guide walking with me too, safety being paramount on all my treks. I am sure that Fran will be a great asset to me on all my future journeys.

MY PRECIOUS STAR

Anne Breach, guide dog puppy walker

As a puppy walker, I am always waxing lyrical to all who will listen about 'my babies'. There are many stories of joy, love and laughter, and the tears when they go back to do their guiding training. However, I could never have anticipated the many tears I would shed when my beautiful Purdie was stolen from the training van and the poor supervisor had to break the news to me.

It was unbelievable that someone could be so cruel. Purdie was about to be matched with a client when this despicable deed was done. However, my faith in human nature was restored when puppy walkers, not only in my area but up and down the country, did everything they could think of to recover Purdie. They walked the streets looking for her, posters were put through doors and put up in vet's surgeries, police stations were visited, common land was combed, etc. etc. I was given so much support from people I hadn't even met.

Purdie became quite a star, appearing in the local newspapers and on the London TV news. I have great faith in prayer and never have I prayed so hard! After 10 weeks I heard from the centre that Purdie had been found in Battersea Dog's Home in London. Thank goodness, all the pups are micro-chipped. A couple of days after her recovery, my husband and I were asked up to the centre to see her. What joy! She was home, rather the worse for wear, but still our same old Purdie. She went absolutely mad when she saw us, and we knew that she would survive.

Survive she did – after lots of TLC and training. She qualified with a gentleman in Oxford. She couldn't be in a nicer home.

We were invited down to see him, and again Purdie showed great pleasure in meeting up with us again. We took Ruby with us, the pup we were walking at the time.

She had the same mum as Purdie, and the two got on really well – but Purdie soon let her know who was top dog!

I shall always have a special affinity with Purdie. To have gone through so much in such a short space of time, and still to have come out on top. She will always be my special star – and I'm sure her owner thinks she is too.

SETTING THE PACE

Bill Smith, guide dog owner

Ely is unique in two ways. As far as we know, he is the only guide dog in the country to have a pacemaker.

Also, he is the only guide dog we know of to work at a college, which means that he has to adapt to being around lots of people all day, every day, and he copes extremely well.

He is playful and friendly to all members of staff and students, and our college wouldn't be the same without him.

It's my pacemaker picking up Radio Three again.

MATCH MAKING

Paddy Wandsborough, guide dog volunteer

Some years ago I had the best Christmas present anyone could ever wish for. I'll tell you about that later, but first I must explain about Rishka!

She was very well 'promoted' to me long before I saw her. Guide Dogs' Neil Ewart phoned me and proudly said: "Have I got a lovely German Shepherd Dog bitch for you!" I told him that I was now too old to have another brood bitch to look after, and I would prefer a nice cheerful little Labrador stud dog to go with my existing GSD stud Tracker who, by then, was nearly 12 years old.

The next time I ventured to the guide dog breeding centre I was told: We've got your bitch. She has been imported from Germany and is in whelp. She's beautiful. Do you want to see her in kennels?"

I pointed out again that I was too old to cope with seasons, matings and puppies, and I would still like a nice little Labrador.

"Oh come, you can't desert your favourite breed," Neil said.

I told him that I had bred Labs long before I had Shepherds and I would like....etc

Of course, in the end I weakened and I went to Rishka when her pups were four weeks old. I did not think she was especially beautiful, but I did think she looked very calm. I was to recall this 'calmness' a few months later when she came to me.

She arrived at my house on a Saturday and seemed to settle in well. The next morning I found she was back in season, so I decided that the Breeding Centre would have to have her for a couple of weeks to escape the amorous attention of Tracker, the stud dog. When she returned, she was more interested in sniffing around the house and, generally, was quite lively. To distract her, I decided to take her out for a walk with Tracker. After a bit of a struggle, we set off at what I can only describe as a gallop.

Rishka obviously loved the walk but wanted to go at her own pace, and she did not care very much if I could not keep up. I knew there had to be one boss, and I informed her that if that boss was not to be me then she could start thumbing a lift back to Germany – or else.

The first thing she had to learn, and quickly, was that she must come when she was called. I started explaining the protocol to her: "Yes, yes. I know. Now let's have a good run!" A long lead, a lot of patience, and an enormous amount of praise when she came, and we progressed little by little. She was very intelligent and quickly learned what I wanted, which, sadly, was not always what she wanted.

I knew about hurricanes, of course, but I had not heard of one called Rishka – she would hurtle towards me. So the next lesson was not just to return, but to immediately sit on arrival. In fact, I had to start puppy walking this four-year-old, headstrong GSD. It was certainly the hardest bit of canine education I had undertaken in over 50 years. She was not over-keen on people, especially men, coming into my house. She would steal anything remotely edible, and I was getting ready to admit failure and send her back to Neil.

I decided to soldier on a little longer, and when she had just passed her fifth birthday I am ashamed to admit that she still tended to pull on her lead. I was advised to try a Halti, something I had never tried before – and it worked.

Then, Rishka had her second litter with me at home.

She was surrounded by love and care. We spent 18 hours together, going through the night, during which time she produced 13 puppies. This was the watershed in our relationship, and a bond of respect and admiration was formed. She was a superb mum, but her flighty ways were not entirely over. After about a fortnight she decided she had done her part and now someone else (me) should look after her pups. I instigated short 'loving sessions' whenever she came to me and told her how wonderful she was. At first she endured them: "That was nice, but let's go out now."

Then she started to come to me for affection, and even gave me sloppy, wet kisses. The house remained 'her' home, but she welcomed anyone in.

So Guide Dogs was right. She was a lovely bitch and there was no return ticket to the Fatherland.

Oh, about that Christmas present. It was the best of all things: love! Just before Christmas, Rishka suddenly gave me hers, fully and trustfully. She lived to a ripe old age and, of course, she was 'beautiful'.

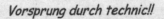

Vorsprung durch technic!!

SILENCE IS GOLDEN

Janet Fairweather, fundraiser for guide dogs

At Christmas, we sang carols outside Twickenham railway station. Two ladies from a local choir also joined us, and our dogs. We were a rather small, select group, so one of the choir ladies plucked up courage to ask one of the ticket collectors to sing with us.

He replied with great feeling: "Madam, if you want to raise money for Guide Dogs, you certainly do not want my voice!"

A BONE TO PICK

Steve Wright, professional falconer and former guide dog instructor

There used to be many things that were supposed to separate us from mere animals. We now know that we are not the only ones to fashion and use tools. Neither do we have a monopoly on the ability to express abstract ideas in speech. We do not have the biggest brain.

One of the first indicators of real intelligence – the ability to reason out a cause and effect in advance – is the telling of lies. Perhaps we have seen a young dog chewing the rug, while its ball lay between its feet. Deceitful, yes; intelligent, perhaps. My story is about one of the cleverest lies I have ever observed in a dog.

We had two Airedale terriers. They were mother and daughter and unlike many of their human equivalents, they rubbed along very amiably with each other. However, tolerant of each other though they might be, and full of bonhomie to the world in general, this good nature did not extend to cats. Both were inveterate cat haters. One of their major roles in life was to ensure that no feline was allowed to enter the garden. If the presence of a cat was even vaguely suspected, they would throw themselves at the French windows (which the older dog could open) and charge up the garden, scattering plants and garden furniture as they went.

Mum was smaller than Toffee, her large pushy daughter, but was very much in charge. They would share food and, on the occasion I am talking about, they had between them a single, new and very juicy marrow bone. It's wrong to say they had it between them, as Mum had purloined it and was selfishly keeping it to herself. What was worse was that she was enjoying it with tremendous gusto.

Her daughter was beside herself with jealousy. She paced the room, moaning piteously to herself and anyone else who would listen. With great tact she would hover as close to her mother as possible, hoping to exploit her generosity. Judging by the growls which this generated from the older dog, you would have said that the milk of canine kindness had worn pretty thin.

What to do? She badly wanted the bone but was powerless to get it. Suddenly in mid-moan she checked and threw herself at the French windows with banshee howls. "There's a cat up the garden! Come quick, there's a cat up the garden!"

Without a second thought, her mother flung herself against the door handle and opened it. With a volley of barks she shot off into the night. Toffee, who prized cat-chasing above all else, quietly turned aside and picked up the bone. There had never been a cat there at all. She had lied, having worked out exactly how her mother would react.

Now that is intelligence!

Some mums never learn.

ON THE BUSES

Maureen Rowley, guide dog owner

Clint has proved very adaptable to the traveling I have to do in and around Bristol, visiting schools and other groups and organisations, giving talks and awareness sessions.

Most days provide a new challenge for him. I usually rely on public transport, catching different buses. Despite this variation, he seems to recognise them and stands up for a 41, 42 and 43 when returning home.

When waiting for a bus the other day, several stopped then continued, with no reaction from Clint. Then a lady said: "He's up! Here's our bus! He can read numbers!"

THERE'S ALWAYS A REASON

Neil Ewart, author

When you are assessing the temperament of a dog it is sensible not to jump to conclusions. A situation I faced many years ago involved a nice Labrador bitch that I was training as a guide dog. She was quite advanced, and was being walked through the middle of Leamington Spa.

Coming towards me was an elderly road sweeper, whom I had met many times, pushing a handcart which contained the rubbish he had collected from the streets. As he approached, the dog started to back away. She seemed to be worried by the human rather than the actual cart, and eventually got into a panic.

This was very much out of character, and she would not respond to verbal or physical encouragement. Even titbits had no effect! Rather than make matters worse, I decided to simply walk on and try and dismiss the incident in her mind.

A few days later, I met the same man, with the same cart, and I was walking the same bitch. This time there was absolutely no problem. I stopped to chat, and asked the man what he thought of the incident.

"Ah well," he said. "I think I know what was wrong. There was a dead cat in the cart. I reckon she could smell it, and it frightened her."

That was surely the answer. My assumption that it was probably the old man himself that had somehow 'spooked' the bitch, was wrong.

She could smell something that upset her, but could not see where it actually was.

If I had not met the old man again, then the assumption that she could be upset by certain humans would have been put on her record.

Dogs can be permanently upset by certain incidents. A rather nasty one I can recollect involved a working guide dog in High Wycombe who was enveloped by a very large plastic sheet.

It was an extremely windy day and the sheet had blown down the street and covered the dog. She did not forget the incident, and showed a lot of concern when working in blustery conditions. Unfortunately, she had to be retired.

EATING THE EVIDENCE

Mike Mason, formerly of the
West Midlands Police Dog Section

On a fine summer morning in June, I reported for duty at 5.45 am.

I was told there had been a number of break-ins in Walsall town centre and, unusually, only foodstuffs had been stolen. Local knowledge told me that this might have something to do with sleepers-out who would now be zonked out in their various places of repose in the Walsall Arboretum (a large local park).

Together with my dog Rinty, I had a look around, and after a short time I discovered a very sleepy group of people in a shed in the park.

I was joined by some colleagues, who had visited the scene of one of the break-ins.

As we were trying to wake the group, we spotted a chocolate cake on a bench close by. "Got you!", we thought. The name of the shop was on the packet.

"You're under arrest," we told them. "Fetch the van, lads, and load them up!"

I turned to collect the very important evidence from the bench – just in time to see the last of the cake together with its packet disappearing down Rinty's throat!

With the evidence gone, and the 'culprits' not admitting anything, we had to let them go.

LONG HAUL HOME

Paddy Wandsborough, guide dog volunteer

One morning we had thick snow and were unable to get to the car to go shopping. We live in the heart of the Cotswolds, miles from any habitation. The sun was shining brilliantly out of a clear blue sky, and all the trees and shrubs were picked out against it.

It was suggested that I should take my camera out with the dogs and get some nice photographs. I told my friend Molly that I was going into the field in the front of the house, just in case anyone was looking for me. Unfortunately, I was to learn later that she did not actually hear what I said!

At the far side of the field there is a stream where, previously, I had got some interesting shots of the sun on water and the hedgerows glistening in ice. I walked around the very edge of the field, avoiding the deep mud, which was now covered by thick snow. At the gate I could see a huge boggy area, but I thought I could jump over it.I soon found out that I could not! I landed in over a foot of very sticky clay and icy water.

I was completely stuck!

I pulled and heaved and wriggled to no avail. Both feet were completely trapped. I then tried to pull my Wellingtons up out of the mud while balancing as best I could on the second trapped foot, but without success. I had nothing to support myself with, and, wobbling perilously, I feared I would be there forever. I began to wonder how long it would be before I might be found. Certainly the farmer would not come into the field as he had his cows under cover because of the snow. No one else came across this field and I knew that Molly could not hear me from the house if I yelled out.

Somehow I had to get out. So now was the time for guide stud dog Tony, a German Shepherd Dog, to come to the rescue. When occasionally I got a stone in my shoes, I had trained Tony to come and lean against me so that I could stand on one foot. So, although I did not have even one foot to stand on, I thought it was worth a go.

Dear, huge, amiable, loving Tony came bounding towards me on command. I hung on to him, and finally managed to get one foot out of a Wellington. We continued to balance on each other as I tried to extricate the boot out of the mud.

With me pulling on the boot and Tony pulling me, we eventually succeeded and I also found myself on firmer ground.

The next project was to try and free the second boot, which remained in glorious isolation in the mud. Despite all my efforts, it would not shift. All that happened was that I fell flat on my face in the mud! I thought that while I was at ground level, I should try to loosen the wretched boot with my hands and actually dig it out. As I lay prone, it crossed my mind that maybe it had been a mistake to discourage Tony from digging in the past. He would have been more effective than I ever could be.

Poor old lad, he really was looking very concerned.

He did seem to know that this was not a game, and he could not understand why I was lying on the dank and filthy ground doing what he was actually forbidden to do. Although it took a very long time, I did free the boot and, with Tony's help, I got back on my feet.

Now the priority was to get back home. Any photos could wait for another time. The distance between me and home was about 300 metres – but the ground was smooth and white, with no indication of what lay beneath. I could not go back the way I had come without re– crossing the bog. I tested every step before taking it, and Tony cleared off with brood bitch, Risk. He loved snow, and he now had a chance to dive-bomb her to get his own back for all the times she pestered him.

But he suddenly decided that I was part of the game and came bounding over to me when, bordering on panic, I cried out to him. However, I was struck down by Tony – and I was stuck again! Incredibly, I got to my feet with his help, but it happened three more times. Each time was more alarming than the previous one.

By this time I was in what can only be described as a 'state'. My language should have melted the snow. On the third descent, I found myself lying on the ground completely stuck. This time, lying on my tummy, I removed the boots. Tony came back, and acting very calmly, he helped me to my feet. The last few yards home were horrific. Luckily, my feet were by now completely dead, so I could not feel lumps of ice and buried stones. Finally, I experienced the huge relief of getting back home.

I was really left with a new understanding of people who are caught in quicksand, and have an enormous sympathy for them. Also, the out-flowing of affection for wonderful, helpful Tony.

WHO DID IT?

Tom Buckley, British instructor of professional dog trainers

For some time now I have been meaning to pass on the definitive answer as to when and where the term

K9 originated. It has certainly caught the imagination of the canine world.

To set the scene, I have to explain that around 1951 the Alsatian Security Services (the earliest known security firms specialising in the use of patrol dogs in the UK, established in 1948) formed a Police Dog Demonstration Team which joined the Gala/Agricultural Show entertainment circuit.

By the late 1960s many police forces had dogs and gave demonstrations at local events and county shows. They did not charge for their services, and we of the Alsatian Security Service were up against unfair competition.

If we were to stay in this branch of 'show business', we had to think of something new. My co-director Ron Darbyshire had been with the War Dog School from its inception – before it was taken over by the Royal Army Veterinary Corps. It occurred to me that we could devise a display format around the lesser known aspects of this type of training.

If we showed how the training was achieved we would not only have an educational and entertaining content, but also preserve some dog training history. To be totally different we would also need a change of name.

We soon came up with the name Commandos (which adequately described the specialist skills required by the dogs and handlers), but it was Ron who remembered that the United States Army had used the code K9 for their original service dogs shortly after they came into the Second World War. He remembered this as he had been responsible for training some of their original dogs. Hence, the K9 Commandos Service Dog Display Team was born.

Sometime in the mid 1970s we did a display at the BBC Sports Club in London. While packing up, we were approached by two smartly attired chaps who showed great interest in our name. They were obviously smitten by the K9 part of it, and thought it was rather clever. We told them the origins and history and duly departed for home.

It was in 1977 that the robot dog named K9 appeared in the Doctor Who series. From that time onwards, the use of the name K9 spread like a rash throughout the land.

Coincidence is a funny old thing!

SUCH A SWEET SOUND

Jenny Moir, head of PR,
Hearing Dogs for Deaf People

Ruffles is a Labrador cross Springer Spaniel, and has been Liz Arendt's hearing dog for nearly nine years.

Very early on in their relationship, Liz realised just how much she would come to rely on Ruffles.

On their first holiday together in a hotel, Ruffles woke Liz on the first night at 4 am. Liz assumed it was because they were in a new environment and told him to go back to bed.

However, he persisted until eventually realisation dawned on Liz that he was trying to tell her that the fire alarm was sounding. After that, Liz learned to trust him implicitly.

Mind you, Ruffles has used his hearing dog

training to benefit himself too! He has taught himself new sounds, including ones that could potentially be to his advantage.

He has discovered that a beeping sound in the kitchen means that Liz has left the fridge door open, so he alerts Liz then leads her to the fridge.

Liz is totally aware this is fast becoming his favourite sound, and that there is an ulterior motive as Ruffles knows that the fridge contains food!

He has also been known to recognise the chimes

BLEEP! BLEEP!

Sniff Sniff

Shall I tell her she's left the fridge door open? Decisions, decisions!!!

from the ice-cream van that comes round their area regularly, and given the chance he will take himself outside and form an orderly queue for his cone!

IGNORANCE IS BLISS

Kim Adrian, Guide Dogs staff

After moving into a new area and buying a German Shepherd called Percy and a Golden Retriever called Sandy, the experience of the first 'long' walk will never be forgotten. They must have been about 10 months old and always came back when called.

We had walked around a field when suddenly both disappeared into woods. After calling for what seemed an eternity – but was probably a few minutes – Sandy appeared.

He sat right in front of us, looking back at the woods and up at us, as much as to say: "It's got nothing to do with me!" We were by this time in the woods on a path, shouting for Percy. After five minutes we heard rustling, and saw emerging from the undergrowth a bow-legged German Shepherd proudly walking towards us with a very large, live chicken in his mouth. Our immediate reaction was: "Oh my God, there's going to be a very irate owner in a minute." But all remained quiet.

One very pleased and proud Percy was told to 'drop' his catch. Much to our surprise, he immediately let go of the chicken, who on contact with the ground, ran for all his worth back the way he had been brought.

As new residents, we didn't want to upset our neighbours, so we cut short the 'long' walk and returned home. We did, however, go for a drink at our local and overheard a regular trying to fathom out why he had a very wet chicken when it hadn't been raining! We have since told the truth and all laughed about it.

NICKING NAMES

Norman McIver, guide dog instructor

A guide dog owner from Northern Ireland recounts this story: she was at a bus stop and told her guide dog Nicki to sit. Then she heard someone tell Nicki to stand, then to sit again. Losing her temper, she remonstrated with the other person for interfering with her dog.

Amazingly, it turned out that the other person was a guide dog owner who also had a dog called Nicki!

SEEING DOUBLE DOBES

Mike Mullan, dog trainer and Kennel Club member

His name was Marcus, a very handsome black and rust Dobermann. Off his property he was always a big softie, but on his own territory he really was the 'Guard Dog Par Excellence'.

Marcus lived about 200 yards down the road from us with his family. There was a six-foot fence right around the whole of the premises, and usually the gates were kept locked so that nobody could enter – even the letterbox was built into the fence.

On this particular summer's day, I had decided to go home for lunch. (I was then the general sales manager of a very large car dealership on the Guildford bypass, about three miles from my house.) About one mile from home, I spied Marcus running loose along the bypass. I stopped the car and called him to me. Without hesitation, he jumped into the car and I took him back to his home.

I went through the then unlocked gate, straight up to the front door, and rang the bell. The door was opened by the lady of the house, and I started to explain that her Dobe had been running loose on the very busy bypass, but I had him safely in the car parked on the drive. As I was talking, the real Marcus suddenly appeared from the back of the garden, showing a full display of his dental equipment! His owner just managed to get him into the house, and I hurried away.

I returned to my car, wondering who my passenger might be – Dobermanns were quite rare in the UK in those days. As I unlocked the door and opened it, I was greeted with my second full dental display in just two minutes! Unfortunately, this time the owner of the teeth was in the car. I could not believe it, as he had been so eager to get into my car and had happily settled down on the back seat as though it was his own – or at least he thought that he actually knew me.

After a few unsuccessful attempts to gain entry to the car, I walked home and had to phone a policeman friend of mine for help. He arranged for two police dog handlers to come to my aid. All was well, and once out of the car the Dobe reverted to being calm and friendly.

After a search, his owners were located. It transpired that the Dobermann had escaped from their car while they were filling up with petrol at a service station on the bypass. There were very pleased to get him back. Some 35 years later, and now a Championship Show judge of the breed, I now know that Dobermanns do not all look the same!

WHAT'S IN A NAME?

Nick Toni, guide dog instructor

Some years ago I trained a dog called Wag at the Bolton centre. All appeared to be going fine in class, but this dog sustained an injury to its tail in the second week (cause unknown), which resulted in him having the tail amputated (poor lad).

Wag did go on to work for many years – just turned out to be an unfortunate name I guess! At least you could never say the tail wagged the dog...

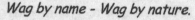

Wag by name - Wag by nature.

DEVIL DOG

PC Steve Dean and Metpol Ashley (now sadly deceased), breeding manager/puppy trainer, Metropolitan Police

Being a police dog handler has been a fantastic job – who else gets paid to go to work every day with their best friend? The duties are, to say the least, very varied.

I have done everything from policing Cup Final football matches to visiting schools, working as part of a SWAT team to performing at Crufts. It's brought me into contact with all sorts of people – from the worst kind of criminal to members of the royal family. But make no mistake, its not all glitz and glamour...

In the part of north London that I patrolled, there is a huge graveyard called Highgate Cemetery. It's famous for two things: the tomb of Karl Marx, and the main entrance being the opening feature in all the old Hammer Horror films.

The cemetery dates back well into the 1700s and has hundreds of tombs and crypts, as well as many gravestones that contain an eternal flame.

Due to its association with horror films – and the sheer size of this cemetery – it's a popular place on Halloween. Every imaginable type of bizarre practice and satanic rite has taken place at this location over the years, including bodies being removed from graves.

It was my misfortune to find myself, along with two colleagues, posted to patrol the grounds of

Highgate Cemetery from 10 pm to 6 am over one Halloween.

It was a typical English, October night. It was cold and and, very much in the tradition of the old Hammer horror films, a slight mist lay just above ground level, swirling and eddying around the gravestones, causing the eternal flames to splutter and flicker in the dark.

The three of us carefully discussed the most effective way to patrol the cemetery grounds. After careful deliberations and much soul searching, we decided that it was in the best interest of everyone concerned, not least ourselves, to remain together – purely on the basis of health and safety you understand. This decision was in no way influenced by the fact that all three of us were scared witless.

We took up our patrol, walking three abreast (not quite holding hands but almost), sticking faithfully to the gravel paths, our dogs walking to heel by our sides.

The night grew eerily quiet as the noise from the surrounding streets settled, broken only by the hooting of a lonely owl.

The three police dogs consisted of one female and two males. In consideration of the fact that my police dog (Ashley) was a widely-used stud and the presence of a female, neutered or not, caused him to become somewhat threatening to other males, we took it in turns to allow the bitch and one or other of the dogs to be off leash at any one time.

As the clock approached 1 am, and with the mist becoming a little heavier, I realised that I had lost sight of my dog. I called out to him in a low voice, mindful of the fact that I was in a graveyard, and you simply don't shout in such places, especially in the middle of the night.

Having got no response, I tried again – but only the bitch responded to the sound of my slightly raised voice, emerging from the gravestones some 15 yards away on to the mist-covered path. I called my dog again, this time a little louder, looking around me for some sign of where the miscreant had got to.

The piercing scream that issued from the graves immediately to our right caused all three of us to act simultaneously in the finest tradition of Scotland Yard's bravest. We screamed back.

It was at this point that the screaming took on a much higher pitch, completely overriding the noise of our confused shouts and commands to the dogs. Suddenly, from the right – and at a speed that would have rivalled Linford Christie – two very odd-shaped figures burst from among the graves.

Both were screaming, but even that didn't drown out what had now become the sound of someone, or something, in abject and mortal terror.

I began to shout the command for my dog to chase and attack, despite not having a clue where my dog actually was. In front of me were two hooded suspects running away and, short of chasing them myself (anyone who knows me will vouch for the fact that I am not built for speed), what else could I do?

The other two police dogs, who were where they should have been – with their handlers – were sent in pursuit and stopped both men within yards. I followed on, still dogless, cursing the fact that I had missed a golden opportunity to give my dog some practical training by letting him chase the two fleeing suspects.

By now the high-pitched screaming had quietened down to a whimper, but it was still audible as we tried to question the two detainees, both of whom were dressed in flowing black robes and hoods. Something had clearly terrified our intrepid duo. One of the men was incapable of making any kind of lucid reply to our questions, repeatedly babbling away to himself, time after time: "Oh no, the devil's got him, the devil's got him." The other man was a little more in control, quickly confessing to being one of three who had entered the graveyard with the intention of practising black magic rites. His story was as follows:

Having climbed over the wall of the cemetery, the three men crept between the graves and tombs, stopping to change into the ceremonial dress of the satanic group that they belonged to. Their intention was to break into one of the old crypts, and perform satanic rites among the coffins.

Disturbed by the sound of our voices, they concealed themselves behind an old tomb, and waited for us to pass by. In a state of intense excitement, as well as fear of being caught, they waited for us to move out of sight. The adrenaline was pumping; their hearts were racing. Alert to every movement and sound, they waited with bated breath.

Suddenly, from around the edge of a tombstone some 30 feet away, there appeared a pair of fiery, red eyes gleaming out of the darkness and mist. On seeing this apparition, one if the trio – now in a

highly nervous state – screamed out: "It's the devil!" and gathering his robes around his waist, broke into a run immediately followed by his two accomplices. All three men, fuelled by terror, were running as fast as they could and screaming as they fled. As they swerved past the tombs and leapt the gravestones, the middle man heard the sound of growling from behind, followed by intense screaming as the beast from hell took down the last man. It was this sound that had clearly carried across the cemetery to us.

Convinced that the "Anti-Christ" was devouring his mate, he ran for his life, leaving his friend to whatever fate the devil had planned for him. It was at this point that they emerged on to the path to be met by the best that the Metropolitan Police had to offer.

Having gleaned this information, I now rapidly made my way towards the sound of the whimpers and snarling. Not, as you might think armed with a clove of garlic and a wooden cross, but with the knowledge that it was a 100 per cent certainty that I was about to discover the location of my missing canine companion. On my arrival, I saw the sorry shape of an ex-devil worshiper, face down in the grass and mud, ceremonial black hood tilted so that it effectively cut of his vision. His ceremonial robes were torn to a shred and his unceremonial white underpants were ripped.

Having taken control of police dog 'Lucifer', aka Metpol Ashley, the now defunct Satanist was arrested under the Ecclesiastical Act of 1860 and conveyed to hospital.

Having been treated and released, and confirmed as being in a fit state of mind, he was charged and subsequently pleaded guilty – no doubt, thanking whatever God he now believed in, for his deliverance from Satan's messenger into the arms of the very kind constable.

The moral of this story is: No matter how hard you train and how imaginative your training scenarios are, you can never cover every eventuality.

FIDGET TAKES FLIGHT

Steve Wright, professional falconer and former guide dog instructor

Jock had escaped the city for a day out with his cousin Harold, a shepherd in a remote Grampian glen. They intended doing some ferreting, and Jock was accompanied, as usual, by Fidget his Jack Russell Terrier. Fidget was good at sniffing out occupied warrens, and was an interested and attentive helper.

The day had gone well and the two men were packing up their nets, ferret boxes and spades, all the while appreciating the beauty that surrounded them. Gazing into the middle distance, Harold suddenly exclaimed: "Hey! There's the eagle".

Sure enough, they could both see the majestic shape cruising along the crest of the hill, its dark plumage blending with the heather whenever it dropped below the skyline.

"It's coming this way. Don't move. It hasn't seen us."

"I think it's spied something. Aye, it's coming into a bit of stoop".

"It's getting closer. It must have seen a hare."

Crouched down in the heather, they watched as the great bird drew closer.Neither of them had ever been this near. Suddenly..

"For **** sake, it's going for Fidget! Here Fidge!"

The warning came too late. One minute quietly pottering about inspecting rabbit holes, and the next seized by sharp and powerful talons and snatched into the air. Fidget's squeal of pain quickly turned to indignation. He was, after all, the descendant of a proud line of doughty workers. Snapping and snarling at his attacker's legs, he fought for his life. The eagle, finding more resistance than it expected – and now frightened off by the shouts and threats from the hitherto unseen men – dropped Fidget at about ceiling height. The little dog bounced safely in the soft heather before running, screaming with fear, to the safety of its owner's legs.

That evening the vet gave Fidget the all-clear, having stitched up a couple of tears and liberally

Drop me off in Torremolinos mate!

applied wound dressing powder. Fidget resumed his life and you would think that nothing had ever happened to him – except that even a sparrow flying over gave him an almighty 'Messerschmitt' twitch.

AND SO TO BED

Norman McIver, guide dog instuctor

A lovely Irishman was starting his training at our centre near Reading. The first introduction to his new dog took place in his bedroom. The trainer asked Paddy (for that was his name) to sit in his chair and do not do anything until the dog actually made physical contact with him.

So, Paddy was left with his new dog, who promptly pulled the duvet off his bed and then shook it vigorously before settling down to lie down in it.

The trainer returned and asked Paddy why he allowed the dog to lie on the duvet. Paddy replied: "It's you who told me to do nothing until the dog actually bothered to make contact with me!"

SNIFFING OUT A SPECIAL GIFT

Neil Ewart, author

History relates many instances of dogs apparently indicating that they have a 'sixth sense'. Examples of dogs finding their way home over vast distances do defy a logical explanation.

However, perhaps we should also remember the numbers that do not return. We know that in many breeds the power of vision is excellent and, of course, hearing, too. What we cannot possibly comprehend is the power of scent. The dog's sense of smell, with its amazing ability to differentiate and identify individual scents, has always fascinated me.

To try and understand how the dog's brain is responding to the myriad of scents being constantly picked up defies me. The brain has to be more complex than the most sophisticated computer, and I often wonder if some of the dogs that perform amazing journeys may, in some way, be using their noses.

I have watched dogs identify the family car in car parks full to the brim. They do not visually recognise the vehicle, but pick it out by the smell. My own German Shepherd Dogs would visit Sussex by the Sea about once year. The old dog adored swimming in the sea.

The journey is nearly 200 miles, but at a certain point outside Hastings he would get up and show extreme signs of anticipation. I do not believe that he actually recognised that particular part of the road, more likely he actually smelt the sea. I should add that it was still a good four miles away.

We do know that the canine nose contains 220 million smell sensitive cells. Compare this to a human, who has only five million smell sensitive cells, and we can begin to appreciate how powerful this sense is in the dog.

A few years ago, I watched a demonstration of drug detection by a Royal Air Force dog. In a mock-up of a house, a quantity of drugs was pushed around the U bend of a toilet (unused I hasten to add!).

A few minutes later, a Labrador sniffer dog was brought in and almost immediately indicated the presence of drugs – even though the scent was passing through water.

Aaaaah! The unmistakable aroma of crack cocaine!

DOG SAVES CAT!

Jenny Moir, head of PR,
Hearing Dogs for Deaf People

Ten-year-old mongrel Scampy has been June Ironside's hearing dog for nearly eight years. She is a gentle dog, and when she went to live with June, she had to share the house with June's elderly Siamese cat, Simon.

Although they took a little while to become friends, Simon eventually warmed to Scampy, revelling in the attention Scampy gave him – especially in the mornings when Scampy would lick him on the cheek to wake him!

Only a few years later, Simon was to owe Scampy his life. One evening when Scampy and June had gone up to bed, Simon came up to join them. After a while he wandered downstairs, as he normally did, and June started to get into bed.

Suddenly Scampy rushed over to her and alerted her with her paw, then ran downstairs as if her life depended on it. June followed her, knowing that something must be terribly wrong.

She found Scampy staring at Simon, and she soon realised that Simon had caught himself on a cord that was hanging on the banisters.

It had wound round his neck, and in trying to free himself he had wound it tighter and was beginning to choke to death. If Scampy had not alerted June so quickly, the consequences would have been tragic.

WATER THERAPY

*Dany Grosemans, Belgian Pet Behaviour Counsellor
and founder of the Belgian centre for guide dogs*

One day I visited a family with a young Jack Russell Terrier. The owners complained about lots of things – the dog showed destructive behaviour, attacked the children (playfully), jumped on visitors, did not obey commands, etc., etc.

While asking more questions about his behaviour, the owners told me that there was one exception. On Fridays, the dog was always fine. He behaved beautifully, and didn't cause any problems. When I asked more detailed questions about the dog's lifestyle, it became clear why he was good one day a week. On Fridays, the mother cleaned the bathroom. While she cleaned the tiles and the sink, she filled the bath with cold water, put the dog in, and let him have a good swim for an hour. The dog enjoyed it thoroughly – and behaved like an angel for the rest of the day.

MOVE OVER!

Derek Coupland, former OIC
Prison Service Dogs

The Prison Service Drug Squad was started in 1972 with a rejected guide dog found for us by the late Derek Freeman (then breeding manager). The dog was basically physically too strong for guide dog work, especially when working in the white harness. When I went to see the dog I liked him very much, and I bought him immediately. Incidentally, I do recall that his breeding was the famous Sandylands strain.

I had not been to the Guide Dogs breeding centre before, and I was very impressed with what I saw. Derek and I got on well, and he later invited me to be a judge at the annual breeders and puppy walkers day held there.

Our National Prison Service Dog Display Team in the 1970's and '80s was, I think, second to none. Our presentation consisted of obedience, agility and criminal work. Depending on the venue, we would also provide a small item of light entertainment.

At the Staffordshire County Show, I met up with Steve Allen (who took over from me on my retirement) and he explained he had something new to try. He said: "When the arena is clear, take a kitchen chair into the middle, sit on it and start reading a newspaper. I will send my dog, Jake (a very large German Shepherd, and I mean large!) to you. He will sit in front of you and bark three times. On the third bark you will stand up and Jake, despite his size, will immediately pinch your seat and perch himself on it.

Please don't forget to move on the third bark!"

I asked what would happen if I didn't.

Steve replied: "He'll do you over!"

Suffice to say I did get up, and he did take over my chair.

There are times when it pays to heed advice.

WHO NEEDS FRIENDS?

Norman McIver, guide dog trainer

A guide dog owner from Edinburgh recounts an incident that occurred when he took his guide dog Becky for a nice free run in a local park. Guide dogs normally wear a leather collar with a medallion and a couple of bells attached, so the location of the dog can be ascertained.

Normally, Becky's recall is excellent. So the owner crossed the road to the park, after first visiting the pub. He put the collar on and let Becky off for her run. After a couple of minutes he whistled her back, and although he could hear the bells it was obvious she was heading in the opposite direction. He tried again, but the sound of the bells suggested Becky was off in another direction. Now he was becoming angry, and the whistle became shriller.

He could hear some laughter and began to smell a rat. His 'pals' had sneaked out of the pub and taken off Becky's collar, and while she looked on with some amusement one of them was running around the park shaking the collar.

A few drams helped renew friendships...

TEETHING TROUBLES

Phil Stott, guide dog instructor

We had an older guide dog owner – we considered him from the old school – who came from a really rough area of Manchester.

He had false teeth which were loose, and when he talked he sounded like a trotting pony. Although he wasn't the most intelligent of gentlemen, he was brilliant at remembering boxing trivia – who fought who, where, when, and the outcome, etc.

On completing a walk just before lunch, we were in the grooming room and I fired a question at him. The answer was Rocky Marciano, and he was so excited as he answered that his teeth shot out on to the grooming room floor.

His dog picked them up, and started to toss them up into the air, playing with them, while his master carried on giving me more details of the fight.

He then reached down, pulled the teeth out of the dog's mouth, and put them straight back into his own mouth – still providing me with details of the referee, and the corner men...

He took his dog into his room and went straight up for his lunch, without cleaning his teeth, and the dog went and had a drink!

MORE ABOUT MARCUS

Mike Mullan, dog Trainer and
Kennel Club member

Behind our house in Guildford was a large recreation park, which was one of the reasons we chose to live there, as it was great for exercising both dogs and children.

Marcus the Dobermann, our near neighbour, was also exercised regularly in this park, so we knew him well. At about 1 am one morning we were awakened by the sound a dog barking incessantly at the entrance gate to the park, which was right by our house. As the noise went on and on, I decided to get up and go and investigate – and there was Marcus, inside the park, barking to be let out. The gates were locked and as I got closer to them, Marcus turned into guard mode!

My intentions had been to go into the park and help him over the gates, but now he was in full attack mode I decided to walk down the road to rouse his owners.

Once at Marcus's home, I explained the situation to the lady owner who agreed to accompany me back up the road to the park. She was only dressed in her nightdress, and I was wearing only my pyjama bottoms – what a sight we made!

We were on a main road with quite a few vehicles travelling up and down it, and all the drivers greeted us with either a wave or a toot on the horn. A resident across the road from the park, who kept the gate key, was awakened by all the noise and came to Marcus' rescue. Once outside with his owner, Marcus again became 'Mr Softie'.

SANTA'S HELPER

Jenny Moir, head of PR,
Hearing Dogs for Deaf People

Sophie is a beautiful Golden Retriever, and she has been Helen Walters' hearing dog since January 2001.

She and Helen often go out raising funds for Hearing Dogs, and on one occasion close to Christmas, in an attempt to appear festive, Sophie had donned a rather attractive headband with red antlers and reindeer ears on it.

She wasn't very impressed at first, until she realised just how much attention it attracted. She looked even cuter than she normally does, drawing quite a big crowd – including a small girl. The little girl approached Helen and tugged at her trouser leg.

When Helen looked down, the girl asked: "Is that a golden reindeer?" Helen, lip reading, nodded and said: "It's a golden hearing reindeer."

The child looked puzzled so Helen explained what a hearing dog does, then finished by saying: "I can't hear so Sophie tells me when Santa Claus has been." The little girl's face lit up in delight and she hugged Sophie, then ran back to tell her Mum about the Golden Hearing Reindeer!

Sophie is very pretty… and she knows it! She is a past master at gaining people's attention, and Helen describes her as a very experienced flirt!

She has already mastered the Marilyn Monroe walk, and if she decides she wants attention from someone who is not co-operating she goes through a blatant "Come up and see me sometime" full siren call to lure people to her side.

It goes like this: first, she makes eye contact; then she gazes wide-eyed at the person with parted lips and a gently waving tail (by now they are hooked!); next she turns sideways on and looks at the person through her eyelashes, then curls all the way round Helen's legs, presenting the person with a view of her bottom (which is swaying as her tail continues to wag); finally, she looks seductively back over her shoulder showing just a little white of eye. The routine never fails!

WAITING GAME

Gary Playfoot, dog handler,
Her Majesty's Prison Manchester

Several years ago I returned from a prison service initial dog handlers' course with a German Shepherd dog called Zeus. He was all black and was still very young – just 12 months old.

One morning I let Zeus out of his kennel, and prepared to take him for his usual morning walk around the fields. Zeus was a highly-strung type and quite excitable at the best of times, but I noticed on this occasion he was even more excited than usual. As I slipped his lead on he was off, pulling me through the gate and out to the path.

Once out on to the pavement, I called him to "heel", and tried to settle him down for the walk to the fields, which normally took a couple of minutes. Well, he was having none of it and attempted to drag me all the way. I can't put up with this, I thought, so I commenced some extra heelwork as I had been taught on my course. "Heel", I commanded, and about-turned to go in the opposite direction. A couple of these manoeuvres followed by ample praise seemed to do the trick.

I soon had his attention, and he settled well to walking to heel. About 100 yards further on, we had to cross the road, so trying to maintain things as they were, I called Zeus to heel and did a smart right turn up to the kerb and told him to sit. Perfect!

I looked both ways to check for traffic. It was all clear, except for a bus some way in the distance. No rush, I thought, it wouldn't do Zeus any harm to be a little patient. As we waited Zeus continued to sit perfectly, but the bus seemed to be getting slower and slower as it approached. I looked down at Zeus, thinking perhaps I was asking a bit too much for him to sit for so long. However, he was doing very well.

The bus was down to a crawling pace, and when it was about 20 yards away, it stopped in the middle of the road. I heard the door open and out popped the driver. He looked up the road the down and turned to me shouting: "It's OK mate, you can cross now, there's nothing coming." For a few seconds I was confused but then the penny dropped. He thought I was trying to cross the road with a guide dog!

Highly embarrassed at the situation I had apparently caused – and not wanting to cause any further scenes – I thanked him and commenced to cross the road. Fortunately, Zeus was spot on as he stuck to my leg like glue, and I was beginning to think I might just get away with it. Wrong! As we reached the other side, I turned left and Zeus promptly turned right.

The ensuing tangle ended up with me in a heap on the floor, with Zeus jumping on me, thinking this was a wonderful game. Needless to say, any dignity I thought I had maintained had now vanished, so I hastily jumped up and sprang into double pace heelwork and disappeared around the first corner I came to.

Zeus soon learned to settle, and he turned into one of the best working dogs and companions I could ever ask for.

MOVING ON

Guide dog puppy walkers

Now you have left us for your training, things don't seem quite the same at home.

Did we mind when you gave yourself a good shake after we had Hoovered, or if you wanted to go out just as Eastenders started? No, we didn't.

Do we miss you? Yes, we do.

The times you have made us laugh trying to carry half a tree trunk in your mouth, or when you snored in unison with your Dad.

What about the times you used to pad out to the wine rack in the kitchen and lick all the empty bottles? That is a habit you will definitely have to get out of – you always did prefer red to white wine...

You are going to have to keep yourself cleaner, as we do not want a repeat of Christmas do we? Just to remind you: Dad took you for a walk on Christmas day with Ian, you rolled in some fox poo, we had to cut short our visit to Canterbury and come home. I spent the next two hours in the van with my head stuck out of the window – you smelt awful.

Please do not worry dear Earl, I am not angry with you for eating two pieces of jigsaw puzzle. You certainly had me fooled, there you were lying down quietly beside me as if butter would not melt in your mouth – and there's me crawling under the table on all fours trying to find the missing pieces.

All we want is for you to do well in your training, take care we love and miss you.

STONE AGE

Norman McIver, guide dog instructor

A guide dog called Ace would carry small stones in from the garden and build up a small store by the fire. Any efforts to remove the pile would result in him going back outside and retrieving them. The guide dog owner would wait until bedtime, close the doors then throw the precious objects way – in the full knowledge that the exercise would be repeated the next day.

I like to think of it as a piece of installation art.

EARLY MORNING RAID

Mike Mason, formerly of the
West Midlands Police Dog Section

Working with the bomb squad, we were sent on an early morning raid in the depths of the countryside. We had information that the IRA had packed a compressor with explosives to be detonated somewhere in the city in the run-up to Christmas, and that this raid was to get to the 'heart of the matter'.

We were with all the top brass from CID and the Crime Squad. I had Paddy the Pointer working as my search dog, and we were the last in a long line of vehicles travelling through villages on a very cold and foggy morning. We pulled into a narrow lane and all the heavy mob, complete with firearms and other equipment, disappeared across a field towards a distant farmhouse. We were told to wait until being called upon to search.

After a few minutes I could hear shouting, and the sound of breaking glass. Then it went very quiet, and shadowy figures could be seen coming across the fields towards me. I could hear mumbles of "Wrong b****y address!"

Back in the van, we continued our journey. The top brass stopped a milkman and asked him the way! Eventually, we arrived at our intended destination. We carried out the search in pouring rain. I checked and made notes of various car registration numbers.

Job done and back to HQ for a debrief. The room was full of the best detectives in the force, and the head asked who took the numbers in the yard. Lots of mutters, nudging and shrugging. I thought: "I'll make them sweat a bit," feeling the bits of paper in my pocket. The boss started to go red in the face.

"I have them," I called out, feeling pleased with myself. "Just leave it to the dog handler – he's always on the ball!"

All eyes turned in my direction with mutterings of "thank God". I then produced a very soggy piece of paper with a very large blue smudge all over it. Everything was totally illegible (well, it was raining at the time!).

Paddy and I made a dash for the door, followed by a tirade of unprintable words, followed by any loose items that could be thrown!

HOT STUFF!

Jenny Moir, head of PR,
Hearing Dogs for Deaf People

Chocolate Labrador Jake has been a hearing dog for profoundly deaf dentist, Pam Willis, since October 2002, accompanying her to her surgery as well as alerting her to household sounds.

In addition to putting Pam's patients at ease, Jake has also averted a possibly tragedy involving Pam's elderly cat Pineau. Pam keeps tortoises, and in the cold winter she brings them inside in a vivarium, which has a heat lamp to keep them warm.

On one occasion Jake alerted Pam with his paw then dropped to the floor, which is the hearing dog's way of indicating danger. After checking the kitchen to ensure that nothing was burning, Pam then looked to find the source of the danger – and what she found astonished her. Unbeknown to anyone, Pineau had sneaked into the tortoise vivarium, and made herself comfortable underneath the heat lamp where she had fallen asleep.

She was totally unaware of the fact that her fur was beginning to singe, which had set the smoke alarm off!

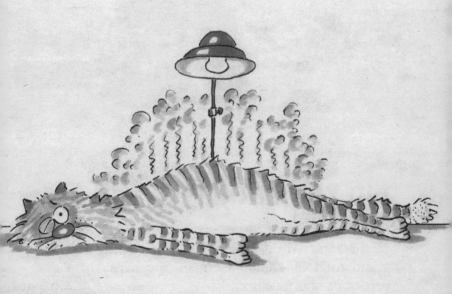

DID YOU KNOW?

In the First World War, the German Army used a grand total of 48,000 German Shepherd Dogs as part of its war machine.

The ancient Greek, Diogenes, was nicknamed 'The Dog' because he flouted social convention and 'embraced shamelessness and poverty.'

Early 17th Century settlers at Jamestown, Virginia used Bloodhounds as guards against hostile Indians.

A GIANT STEP FOR THE VET

Dr Andrew Edney, Vet

Its always very awkward when friends get divorced and you want to stay friendly with both. Two such were dog breeders and they had nine dogs.

After much discussion and argument, they apportioned their canine companions as best they could, that is they kept four each. This left the ninth, which had not been allocated.

They brought this bitch of rising six years into my surgery and told me the situation. Much as they were reluctant to do so, they had decided that euthanasia was the only sensible course of action for Nina.

I had only been in practice about two years but had come to realise that one must not become too emotionally involved with sad situations or you would soon become a physical and mental wreck. On the other hand veterinarians must never be seen to be totally insensitive.

I thought I had learnt where to position myself. However, this was different, these were real friends and I knew all their dogs individually. After much anguish, I just came out with it: "I can't do that, it's like killing a person."

"OK," they replied "Either you put her down or take her on".

If you took on all the animals you felt sorry for in veterinary practice you would soon be over-run; but I did this time and I'm pretty sure they knew I would.

In the event it was a marvellous success. Although Nina only lived for about three more years, she clearly saw me as her hero! She had a sense of humour and we had many hilarious adventures. Nina was an Irish Wolfhound, and she was nearly as big as me.

Where we lived there were some twenty Miniature Dachshunds and she would bound around as if she was one of them.

I would go down the pub with her and a handful of Dachs on leads, which always invited ready comment. She would clear away any food high on the bar.

I would take her on calls with me, and one day whilst negotiating a sharp bend she broke the side window as she put her hefty shoulder through it.

It was practically impossible to walk down the street with her without people coming up to ask me what she was, and most times making silly comments. "Oh it's an Airedale cross isn't it?" "She's as big as a donkey!" and so on.

In the end I had a disk made with I AM AN IRISH WOLFHOUND clearly engraved thereon. I still have it.

Sadly giant breeds are not long lived, and she died of a pancreatic tumour and only just made it past eight years.

But I will always remember that "You are never alone with an Irish Wolfhound!"

Joking Apart

Those of us who have worked in veterinary practice are well used to patients who give their pets strange names. I had a clergyman client with a cat called Magnificat and a Greek scholar with one he named Oedipuss.

One day we were filling in the card for a new client with a rather cute-looking puppy of rather indeterminate ancestry. "Name?" I asked. "Joker" was their response. "No, I want your name not the dog's".

"It is Mrs Joker" she said sharply, to my acute embarrassment.

Misalliance

Of all the crossbred dogs I have encountered, one remains a special memory. It was a very strange-looking animal.

The owner had been asked so many times what it was, she volunteered the information without waiting to be questioned.

"It's a cross between a Standard Poodle and a Miniature Dachshund, and it happened on the stairs!"

ODE TO KARL

Guide dog puppy walkers

For a Guide Dogs puppy walker, the day that a pup successfully completes its puppy walking, and leaves to begin its training, can be filled with mixed emotions . . .

THERE'S SOMETHING MISSING

I haven't had to Hoover today
And I haven't tripped over any bones
There are no twigs scattered over the floor
There's something missing today

No one has followed me up the stairs
The dishwasher is open and no one appeared
There are no dirty towels on the line
There's something missing today

My rose still has all its blooms
And all the pebbles in the pond are in place
No toys have been dumped at my feet
There's something missing today

I haven't been to the park for days
And no one wants their tummy tickled
Your "dad" hasn't said how handsome you are
There's something missing today